Cardinal Publishers Group
USA Distributor
2402 N. Shadeland Ave., Suite A
Indianapolis, IN 46219
317-352-8200 –ph
317-352-8202 –fx
www.cardinalpub.com

First Published 2018

© Australian Fishing Network
Australian Fishing Network
PO Box 544 Croydon, Victoria 3136
Telephone: (03) 9729 8788   Facsimile: (03) 9729 7833
Email: sales@afn.com.au   Website: www.afn.com.au

ISBN 8 54935 006268

Design and production by Australian Fishing Network
Illustrations by Trevor Hawkins

Printed in China

USA
FRESHWATER
FISH
GUIDE

CHAD FOSTER & TREVOR HAWKINS
ILLUSTRATIONS TREVOR HAWKINS

The USA's world of freshwater is plentiful with all shapes and sizes of fish, from tiny transparent glass minnows to the giant armor plated alligator gar exceeding 300 pounds. Freshwater lakes, streams, rivers, canals, and sloughs are so wide spread, no matter what your GPS coordinates read your bound to be near fishable freshwater. With the abundance of species available, it's not out of the question to be pleasantly surprised with an unidentifiable catch.

This book provides information on nearly all USA's freshwater fish species and written in a language everyone can apply in the field. You'll find range, habitat, description, size, edibility, game status, and best of all, fishing tips any angler may incorporate into his/her bag of tricks. This book will be a useful addition to the bookshelves of the keen and occasional recreational fisher in the USA.

Fishing is a rapidly growing sport from coast to coast. With an influx of anglers feeling the desire to battle their next trophy fish or harvest a quality meal, all anglers must take these environmental factors in consideration.
Practice catch and release.
If you want to mount a fish, take pictures, release the fish, and get a replica mount.
While fishing for the table, only keep medium to small size fish. Adults are the main reproducers for the next generation.
Be aware and follow rules and regulations.
Dispose of all trash properly.
If everyone works as a team and follows these few factors, our sport will be around for generations to come.
Thanks for reading and enjoy the book.

Chad Foster

INDEX

Acara, black 5
Alewife 5
Bairdiella 5
Bass, guadelupe 6
Bass, hybrid (sunshine bass) 6
Bass, largemouth 7
Bass, ozark 7
Bass, redeye 8
Bass, roanoke 8
Bass, rock (northern rock bass) 9
Bass, shadow 9
Bass, shoal 10
Bass, smallmouth 10
Bass, spotted 11
Bass, striped 11
Bass, suwannee 12
Bass, white 12
Bass, yellow 13
Blackfish, sacramento 13
Bluegill 14
Bonytail 14
Bowfin 15
Buffalo, bigmouth 15
Buffalo, black 16
Buffalo, smallmouth 16
Bullhead, black 17
Bullhead, brown 17
Bullhead, snail 18
Bullhead, spotted 18
Bullhead, yellow 18
Burdot 19
Carp, bighead 19
Carp, common 20
Carp, grass 20
Catfish, blue 21
Catfish, channel 21
Catfish, flathead 22
Catfish, walking 22
Catfish, white 23
Char, arctic 23
Chub, lake 24
Chub, creek 24
Chub, dixie 24
Chub, hornyhead 25
Chub, humpback 25
Chub, roundtail 26
Chubsucker, creek 26
Chubsucker, lake 26
Cichlid, mayan 27
Cichlid, midas 27
Cichlid, peacock 28
Cichlid, rio grande 28
Cisco 29
Crappie, black 29
Crappie, white 30
Dolly varden 30
Drum, freshwater 31
Drum, red 31

Eel, american 32
Fallfish 32
Flier 33
Flounder, southern 33
Gar, alligator 34
Gar, florida 34
Gar, longnose 34
Gar, shortnose 35
Gar, spotted 35
Goby, round 36
Goldeye 36
Goldfish 37
Grayling, arctic 37
Guapote, jaguar 38
Hardhead 38
Herring, blueback 39
Herring, skipjack 39
Inconnu 40
Killifish, banded 40
Ladyfish 40
Lamprey, sea 41
Minnow, sheepshead 41
Mooneye 42
Mullet, striped 42
Mummichog 43
Muskellunge 43
Muskellunge, tiger 44
Needlefish, atlantic 44
Oscar 44
Paddlefish 45
Peamouth 45
Perch, sacramento 46
Perch, silver 46
Perch, white 47
Pickerel, chain 47
Pickerel, redfin 48
Pike, northern 48
Pikeminnow, colorado 49
Pikeminnow, northern 49
Pikeminnow, sacramento 49
Pikeminnow, umpqua 50
Pumpkinseed 50
Quillback 50
Redhorse, blacktail 51
Redhorse, golden 51
Redhorse, river 52
Redhorse, shorthead 52
Sailfin molly 53
Salmon, atlantic 53
Salmon, chinook 54
Salmon, chum 54
Salmon, coho 55
Salmon, kokanee (landlocked sockeye salmon) 55
Salmon, pink 56
Salmon, sockeye 56
Sculpin, fourhorn 57
Sculpin, mottled 57
Sculpin, slimy 58

Seatrout, spotted 58
Shad, alabama 59
Shad, american 59
Shad, gizzard 60
Shad, hickory 60
Shad, threadfin 60
Shark, bull 61
Sheepshead 61
Shiner, emerald 62
Shiner, golden 62
Shiner, river 62
Silverside, atlantic 63
Silverside, brook 63
Silverside, inland 63
Sleeper, bigmouth 64
Smelt, longfin 64
Smelt, rainbow 64
Snakehead, chevron 65
Snapper, gray 65
Snook, common 66
Snook, swordspine 66
Snook, tarpon 67
Steelhead 67
Stingray, atlantic 68
Stonecat 68
Sturgeon, atlantic 68
Sturgeon, green 69
Sturgeon, lake 69
Sturgeon, pallid 70
Sturgeon, shortnose 70
Sturgeon, shovelnose 71
Sturgeon, white 71
Sucker, blue 72
Sucker, flannelmouth 72
Sucker, longnose 73
Sucker, white 73
Sunfish, green 74
Sunfish, longear 74
Sunfish, redbreast 75
Sunfish, redear 75
Sunfish, spotted 76
Tarpon 77
Tilapia, blackchin 76
Tilapia, blue 77
Tilapia, mozambique 78
Tilapia, redbelly 78
Tilapia, spotted 78
Tilapia, wami 79
Tomcod, atlantic 79
Trout, brook 80
Trout, brown 80
Trout, bull 81
Trout, cutthroat 82
Trout, golden 82
Trout, lake 83
Trout, rainbow 83
Warmouth 84
Whitefish, lake 84

Whitefish, mountain 85
Whitefish, round 85

Rigs Bass
Carolina Worm Rigs 86
Vertical Carolina Rig 86
Texas Rigs 86
Topwater Baits 86
Crankbait 86
Split Shot Rig 87
Drop Shot Rigs 87
Spinner Baits 87

Rigs Walleye
Leech Rig 88
Bottom Walking Rig 88
Stand up Jig and Nightcrawler 88

Rigs Crappie & other Panfish
Double Spreader Rig 89
Jig and Float Rig and Bobber and Meal Worm Rig 89
Double Bear Paw Rig 89

Rigs Pike-Pickerel & other Large Gamefish
Weedless Spoon Rigs 90
Bottom Bumping Rig 90
Weedless Live Bait Rig 90
Quick Set Rig 90
Controlled-Depth Live Bait Rig 90

Rigs Sturgeon
Slider with Shrimp Rig 91
Slider Rig with Half Hitched Smelt 91
Sewn Shad Sturgeon Rig 91
Bank Breakaway Rig 91
Soft Bottom Estuary Rig 91

Rigs Salmon
Delta Diver & Salmon Bungee 92
Delta Diver & Spinner Rig 92
Spin-N-Glo Rig 92
Basic Plunking Rig 92
Deepwater Bobber Float Rig 93
Anchored Boat Rig 93
Back Bouncing Plugs 93
Basic Prawn Trolling Rig 93

Rigs Steelhead
Pencil Lead Cinch 94
Double Hook Side - Drifting Rig And Slinky 94
Float Fishing Rigs 94
Diver and Bait Rigs 95
Side-Planer Rigs 95
Spawn Sac Rig 95
Pink Plastic Worm Rig 95

Rigs Trout and Kokanee Rigs
Trolling Rig 96
Bottom Rig 96
Float Rigs 97
Down Rigger Setups 97

ACARA BLACK

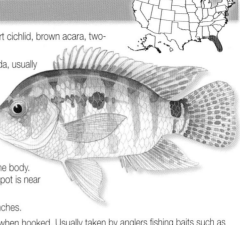

Scientific name: Cichlasoma bimaculatum. Also known as port cichlid, brown acara, two-spotted cichlid, two-spot cichlid.

Range: Not native to the USA. Now found throughout south Florida, usually in disturbed or altered habitat. As far north as Jacksonville.

Habitat: Usually throughout smaller freshwater canal systems and swampy locations. Shallow, stagnant ditches and gutters. Infrequent in larger lakes and canals.

Description: Stout, bream-looking fish with a convex shaped head. Similar in shape to the Oscar. Color is variable, from gray/silver/whitish to brown. Often has blue/green sheen. Most noticeable features are the two blotches along the side of the body. The forward blotch located mid-body is the largest. The smaller spot is near the tail. The dorsal and anal fins are pointed at the rear.

Size: Maximum weight is around 4 ounces and length to eight inches.

Tackle and fishing: A sprightly but not overly strong little fish when hooked. Usually taken by anglers fishing baits such as worms from poles. Will take very small flies and jigs occasionally.

Edibility: N/A. Too small.

Game status: N/A. Too small.

ALEWIFE

Scientific name: Alosa pseudoharengus. Also known as freshwater herring.

Range: Gulf of St.Lawrence and Northern Nova Scotia to North Carolina.

Habitat: Close to shore waters and moving into freshwater rivers to spawn. Landlocked populations exist in Lake Ontario and other large northern lakes.

Description: Typical herring colors. Grayish green above with pale silver sides and belly. Flanks are iridescent green violet and the upper flanks are faintly striped with longitudinal lines in bigger fish. A dusky spot behind the gill cover.

Size: Grow to 15 inches in length but average about 10-11 inches and 9 ounces in weight.

Tackle and fishing: Not recognised for its fighting ability. Rarely caught on rod and line. Mostly taken in nets.

Edibility: Very good.

Game status: N/A.

BAIRDIELLA

Scientific name: Bairdiella icistia. Also known as Ronco croaker, corvineta ronco, ronco roncacho.

Range: Gulf of California, Mexico to Nicaragua. Introduced successfully into the Salton Sea in southern California where it is a popular sportfish.

Habitat: A demersal species inhabiting coastal waters and estuaries to depths of around 60 feet. Often close to shore around structure, surf beaches and gutters. Sometimes in lower rivers.

Description: Overall silver with a large spine on the leading edge of the anal fin. This fin distinguishes the fish from the Corvinas that it may be confused with.

Size: Normally found around 6-8 inches. Can achieve twice that length.

Tackle and fishing: Too small to offer any great fight but fun to catch; especially on ultra light spin tackle. Often caught with poles or handlines using shrimp, cut squid or baitfish and other marine baits.

Edibility: Excellent.

Game status: Good fun. Best on ultra light tackle.

BASS, GUADELUPE

Scientific name: Micropterus treculi. Also known as black bass, Guadelupe spotted bass.

Range: Only occurring in Texas, and is that states official fish. Found in the Guadelupe River above Gonzales, headwaters of the San Antonio River, and the Colorado River north of Austin.

Habitat: Deep pools and eddies in small fast flowing rivers. Around rocks, stumps and similar structure.

Description: Generally green in color and similar to the spotted bass. The darker bands however are bigger, darker and more mottled in appearance. The flank coloration also extends further down the body than it does on the spotted bass.

Size: Usually less than 12 inches in length. World record is 3 pounds 11 ounces. IGFA All-Tackle World Record 3 pound 11 ounces, Lake Travis, TX, USA.

Tackle and fishing: A good fighter for its small size. Best sport is achieved by using ultra light spin or fly tackle. They will hit artificial worms, jigs, crankbaits and flies. They will also eat natural baits such as night crawlers, minnows and crawfish.

Edibility: Very good. Most fish caught are released however.

Game status: Very good. On ultra light tackle.

BASS, HYBRID [SUNSHINE BASS]

Scientific name: Morone saxatilis x chrysops. Also known as wiper, whiterock bass, hybrid bass.

Range: Sunshine bass are hybrids between striped bass (morone saxatilis) and white bass (morone chrysops) and as such don't have a natural geographic range. They are widely stocked across the southern states.

Habitat: Tend to occupy deeper waters and holes similar to its parent fish, although it does come to the surface when chasing baitfish.

Description: Very similar to both its parent fish although most easily recognised by the broken and irregular lines along the body.

Size: A fast growing fish that regularly reaches 8-10 pound and occasionally larger. Maximum size around 16 pound.

Tackle and fishing: A very aggressive feeder that is recognised by anglers for its hard-fighting antics when hooked on light spin and baitcasting outfits. Popular lures include bucktail jigs, soft plastic fish imitations, crankbaits, spoons and other lures that imitate shad. Fish baits such as shad, shiners and minnows are popular.

Edibility: Very good.

Game status: Very good.

BASS, LARGEMOUTH

Scientific name: Micropterus salmoides. Also known as bigmouth bass, green bass, black bass, Oswego bass, bayou bass, bucket mouth, line side, lake bass. There are two recognised subspecies, northern largemouth bass (Micropterus salmoides salmoides) and the Florida largemouth bass (Micropterus salmoides floridanus).

Range: Now established in all sates except Alaska. The original range was mostly the eastern half of the United States.

Habitat: All water types, including rivers, creeks, ponds, swamps and lakes. They prefer weedy and clear waters and are also found in estuaries in certain areas. They are rarely found in water deeper than 19 feet, moving to deeper (warmer) water in winter and back into the warmer shallows in spring.

During daylight hours they lie around structure such as lily pads, piers, overhanging brush and trees or cruise above shallower submerged weed beds. During the night they retreat to deeper water and lie up on the bottom or amongst logs and structure.

They prefer warm water temperatures ranging between 81-86 degrees Fahrenheit.

Description: A large, slightly upward sloping mouth and upper jaw that extends past the point of the eye. The body is solid and slightly compressed laterally. Generally overall olive green in color that can be pale or almost black depending on the environment the fish is living in. The lower body and underside of head is lighter and the belly whitish. There is a prominent, blotchy striped pattern running from the eye to the centre of the tail. Eye coloring is golden brown.

Size: Most fish average 18 inches. Between 1-3 pounds in weight is averange, but fish of twice this size aren't uncommon. IGFA All-Tackle World Record 22 pound 4 ounces, Montgomery Lake, GA, USA.

Tackle and fishing: One of the most popular and sort after freshwater sportfish in the United States. They an aggressive fish that will hit lures, flies and baits with equal enthusiasm. They are an acrobatic fish that offer a strong fight, especially on lighter outfits.

Fishing outfits should reflect where you're fishing. In amongst snags and weedbeds it may be necessary to use heavier lines and stronger outfits to subdue and turn larger fish.Artificial lures such as plastic worms, spinners, top water plugs and jigs are all successful. Fly anglers often use surface popper flies.

Fishing live baits such as crawfish, leeches, frogs, minnows and night crawlers are all successful in various regions of the country.

Edibility: Fair/Good. Flesh is moderately firm and mild. The water from which the fish is caught usually determines eating quality. Often eats best when skinned.

Game status: Excellent. An iconic sportfish.

BASS, OZARK

Scientific name: Ambloplites constellatus. Also known as rock bass.

Range: Native only to the White River area of Arkansas and Missouri. Common in its range. Introduced into non-native drainages such as the Osage River (Missouri). None of these introductions seem to have established self-sustaining populations.

Habitat: Prefer clear pools in permanently flowing small,rocky highland creeks and small rivers. Found around rocks, logs, banks and vegetation. Found in a few clear water reservoirs.

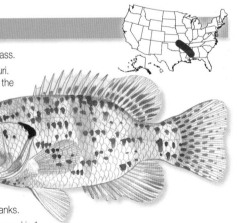

Description: Similar to rock bass and other close relatives. A close cousin (different coloring) to the shadow bass, which inhabits different drainages in Arkansas. Best distinguished by the numerous small dark dots scattered over the flanks.

Size: A small fish that generally weighs less than 8 ounces. World record is 1 pound.

Tackle and fishing: A popular and scrappy little fighter but too small to offer any resistance. Mostly caught with poles or on ultra light fly or spin tackle. They feed on insects and crayfish. Can be caught on worms, aquatic insects, and small minnows. They will also take artificial nymphs, popping bugs and very small lures.

Edibility: Very good.

Game status: Good. Mostly targeted for a feed.

BASS, REDEYE

Scientific name: Micropterus coosae. Also known as Coosa bass.

Range: Entire range is limited to Georgia, Alabama and small areas of South Carolina and Tennessee. The Mobile basin Alabama, Coosa and Tallapoosa drainages.

Habitat: Rivers and streams with a lot of structure such as boulders, submerged logs, vegetation and undercut banks. They prefer a moderate current flow and mostly rocky areas of the stream. They can be found in several upstate South Carolina impoundments.

Description: A slender bodied bass with a bronze/olive body coloring fading to white on the belly. Dark vertical blotches along the flanks and horizontal rows of spots on the lower side. The tail is red or orange and the anal fin has an orange margin. Eye is red. The mouth extends to the rear of the eye but not beyond.

Size: Average length is 6-9 inches. In streams most fish would weight 6-8 ounces and in lakes 1 pound. Rarely exceeds 2 pounds.

Tackle and fishing: A scrappy and acrobatic fighter when taken on very light spin, baitcasting or fly tackle. Their natural food items are terrestrial and aquatic insects, crayfish, small baitfish and salamanders. Worms, small crawfish and small minnows are popular natural baits. Small plastic worms, in-line spinners and small surface plugs are used. Fly fishers use dry and wet flies, streamers and small surface popping bugs.

Edibility: Very good.

Game status: Very good. On very light tackle.

BASS, ROANOKE

Scientific name: Ambloplites cavifrons. Also known as perch, rock bass, redeye.

Range: Occurs only in the Roanoke River and Chowan River drainages in Virginia, and the Tar and Neuse River drainages in North Carolina. There is concern for its future due to dams and environmental damage to its native rivers.

Habitat: Inhabits streams, large creeks and small rivers that flow clear. They prefer deep, swiftly flowing runs around rocks and over gravel. They inhabit the heads of pools. Sometimes found in more turbid water and swamps.

Description: Similar robust body like the rock bass. Coloring is olive green/olive brown on the back fading to gray on the flanks and white bellow on the belly. Have small spots on the scales (smaller than rock bass) and small yellow or white spots on the upper body and head.

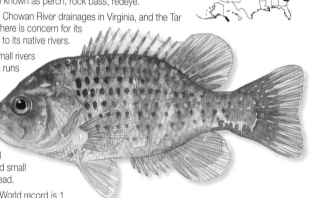

Size: Half a pound or less is the average size. World record is 1 pound 5 ounces.

Tackle and fishing: A scrappy little fighter that mostly feeds on crustaceans, minnows and crayfish. Usually targeted by anglers using poles, ultra light spin or fly tackle. They will take natural baits such as worms, small minnows and crayfish, flies and small lures such as crankbaits, spoons and spinnerbaits.

Edibility: Very good.

Game status: Good. On very light tackle

BASS, ROCK [NORTHERN ROCK BASS]

Scientific name: Ambloplitesrupestris. Also known as redeye, black perch, rock sunfish, rock perch, goggle-eye.

Range: Native to east-central North America. Widely introduced in many areas. A commercial fish species in the Great Lakes.

Habitat: Throughout rocky areas in lake shallows. In many smallmouth bass waters in flowing streams, in pools and around rocky structure. Adults live in groups.

Description: Often confused with shadow bass, Roanoke bass and Ozark bass. This is the largest and has a robust body. Rock bass are most easily identified by the fact they have six spines on the anal fin (others in the group have three). Coloring is dark green/olive overall with darker blotches along the flanks and rows of small dark dots below the lateral line. They change color to suit their habitat however.

Size: A quick growing fish that averages 6-8 inches in length. Some reach 12 inches, but they rarely reach more than 1 pound in weight. IGFA All-Tackle World Record 3 pound, York River, Ontario and 3 pound, Lake Erie, PA, USA.

Tackle and fishing: A very aggressive little fish that fights hard for its size and hits numerous baits, artificial lures and flies. Anglers use poles, spin and fly tackle when chasing these fish. Natural baits include worms, minnows and cut baits. Small jigs and spinners are successful as are popping bugs and streamer flies.

Edibility: Very good. Their flesh is firm and extremely tasty.

Game status: Very good. For its diminutive size.

BASS, SHADOW

Scientific name: Ambloplites ariommus. Also known as rock bass.

Range: Native to Mississippi, Missouri, Arkansas, Georgia and Louisiana. It is most common in Florida, Georgia, Louisiana, Mississippi and Alabama.

Habitat: It inhabits small, to medium sized cool flowing rivers and streams similar to those preferred by smallmouth bass. It prefers slow flowing water flowing over sand, gravel, pebbles and silt-free mud bottoms. It likes bushy undercut banks and vegetated pools where its main diet consists of crayfish and other small invertebrates.

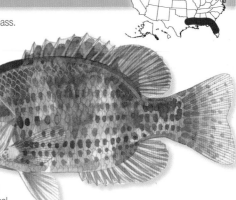

Description: A large mouthed fish with the upper jaw extending to the middle of the eye. Overall coloring is usually light brown or olive overall overlaid with two to four darker brown vertical blotches or 'shadows'. The eye is red/reddish orange and very large. Has the ability to change its coloration to match its environment.

Size: Rarely larger than one half pound. Mostly 6-8 inches in length. World record is 1 pound 13 ounces caught in Arkansas.

Tackle and fishing: A scrappy little fighter on ultra light tackle. Usually taken with poles or spin tackle using worms, crickets, minnows, in-line spinners and jigs.

Edibility: Very good.

Game status: Good.

BASS, SHOAL

Scientific name: Micropterus cataractae. Also known as Redeye bass, Flint River smallmouth.

Range: Native to subtropical waters in Florida and Georgia.

Historically from the Apalachiola River, but no longer in the river proper due to habitat destruction. Chipola River system in Florida. The Flint and Chattahoochie River systems of Alabama and Georgia.

Habitat: Most commonly associated with rock shoals and uncommon in other habitats.

Description: Similar in shape to largemouth bass, and often confused with redeye bass. Dark green body coloring, with distinctive dark vertical stripes above the midline of the body. Belly is cream or white. No red or orange on tail or anal fin as in the redeye bass, the tails are dark green or black, but the eye is red. Upper jaw does not extend past the eye as it does in largemouth bass.

Size: Average 1-2 pound. Anything around 2 pound or larger is considered a big fish.

IGFA All-Tackle World Record 8 pound 12 ounces, Apalachicola River, FL, USA.

Tackle and fishing: Pound for pound one of the best fighters in the bass family. Light spin, baitcasting and fly tackle are mostly used to catch these tough fighting fish. Soft crawfish, grub and worm imitations are popular, as are small spinner baits, crankbaits, jerkbaits and surface plugs. The most popular natural baits are worms, minnows and crawfish. Flyfishing for shoal bass is popular due to the environments the fish inhabit.

Edibility: Good. Flesh is white and flaky but tends to be drier than that of largemouth or redeye.

Protected in places and vulnerable. Consider releasing all fish to protect the species.

Game status: Very impressive.

BASS, SMALLMOUTH

Scientific name: Micropterus dolomieu. Also known as smallmouth, brown bass, bronzeback, smallie, bronze bass.

Range: Native to the Hudson Bay basin, Saint Lawrence River system and the upper and middle Mississippi River basin. Heavily transplanted and now in all states except Alaska, Louisiana and Florida.

Habitat: Prefers cooler water temperatures than Largemouth bass. It also prefers clearer (flowing) waters of streams and rivers and prefers sandy (less weedy areas) lakebeds, especially around rock and submerged tree structure.

They prefer clean, unpolluted water.

Description: Mostly brown (bronze) dorsally with paler brown/ greenish flanks overlaid with dark vertical bands. Belly is pale yellow/white. The upper jaw only extends back to be in line with the middle of the eye.

The habitat in which they live usually influences their coloration.

Size: Most fish taken average around 1-2 pounds. Fish of twice this weight aren't rare. Male fish are generally smaller than females.

IGFA All-Tackle World Record 10 pound 14 ounces, Dale hollow, TN, USA.

Tackle and fishing: A very good (one of the best) fighting fish that is both strong and acrobatic. Because they tend to prefer open water areas they can be targeted using lighter tackle that also allows them to put up a better fight. They eat various foods including frogs, insects, crayfish and even small mice.

They are usually fished for with light spin and baitcasting tackle as well as fly tackle where appropriate. They can be caught on a range of natural and artificial baits and lures. Jigs, crankbaits, spinnerbaits, plastic jerkbaits are all productive as are various wet and dry flies.

Natural baits as mentioned above are all successful.

Edibility: Excellent. Fillets are white and firm when cooked. Most fish are released however.

Game status: Excellent. The best of all the freshwater bass.

BASS, SPOTTED

Scientific name: Micropterus punctulatus. Also known as Kentucky bass, Alabama spotted bass, black bass, redeye, spotty, spots.

Range: Native to the Mississippi River basin and across the Gulf states. Has been introduced into western North Carolina and Virginia.

Habitat: Prefer streams and rivers with clear, long pools with slow moving water over gravel or rock bottoms. They avoid shallow and heavily vegetated areas. They also inhabit cool water reservoirs and lakes and can be found mostly around steep dropoffs. They frequent deeper water than other freshwater bass species.

They prefer clean, unpolluted water.

Description: Very similar to largemouth bass but with a smaller mouth. Elongated body. Green dorsally and yellow to white below. A horizontal line of interconnected dark blotches running from the eye to the start of the tail. The lower flanks have rows of horizontal dark spots from which the fish gets its name. Smaller fish often have a darker blotch immediately in front of the tail. The upper jaw only extends to the rear edge of the eye, not past it as in largemouth bass.

Size: Average around one pound. Two pounders are good fish.

IGFA All-Tackle World Record 10 pound 4 ounces, Pine Flat Lake, CA, USA.

Tackle and fishing: A strong and at times acrobatic fighting fish when taken on light tackle. Similar fishing techniques and tackle as for smallmouth bass.

Edibility: Excellent.

Game status: Excellent. On light tackle.

BASS, STRIPED

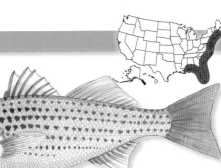

Scientific name: Morone saxatilis. Also known as Rock bass, striper, rockfish, linesider, striper bass, squidhound, streaked bass.

Range: From Nova Scotia to North Florida along the Atlantic coast,and most prevalent from Maine to North Carolina. Only along the north coast of the Gulf of Mexico. British Columbia to northern Baja California, Mexico.

Habitat: Striped bass are found in coastal waters as well as in rivers and lakes. A migratory fish that travels between fresh and saltwater to spawn although landlocked populations also exist and don't need to migrate to successfully spawn. They inhabit coastal waters and bays and can be found up to 10 kilometres offshore.

Recognised as a prime surf species although regularly caught in bays, coastal shores and rivers, as well as over closer offshore reefs and rips. Regularly targeted around rocky points, especially where there is rough water and currents and where shallow and deep waters converge.

Description: Solidly built fish with a dark green/gray dorsal area, with silver sides and belly and distinctive longitudinal stripes along the body. These stripes are regularly spaced and unbroken.

Size: Average sizes taken by anglers range between 5 and 20 pound although it can reach 4 feet and 90 pound and beyond on occasions.

IGFA All-Tackle World Record 78 pound 8 ounces, Atlantic City, NJ, USA.

Tackle and fishing: A very popular sportfish that fights strongly and offers a tough challenge, especially when hooked in areas where there are strong flowing currents.

Striped bass are fished for with all categories of casting tackle, depending on the location where these fish are sought. Smaller to medium sized fish offer good sport on spinning, fly and baitcasting tackle, while bigger specimens are often tackled with similar, but stouter outfits that allow anglers to fish live baits, troll, spin or surf cast.

Natural baits often include smaller baitfish, dead or alive, crab, eel or marine worms as well as cut baits.

Various lures such as feathers, spoons, surface and swimming plugs and poppers are all used, and the type and size will often depend on whether anglers are trolling or casting from a boat or shore, as well as water conditions encountered. Streamer and popper flies are popular when fly anglers are fishing calmer or generally shallower areas and flies that resemble the local baitfish are most productive.

Edibility: Very good.

Game status: Very good.

BASS, SUWANNEE

Scientific name: Micropterus notius.

Range: Originally only found in Suwannee and Ochlockonee Rivers. In North Florida and South Georgia. Now in the Santa Fe, Ichetucknee, St. Marks, Aucilla and Wacissa systems.

Habitat: They have a preference for rapidly flowing water over rocky substrate. Found away from the edges, down deep in rock strewn pools.

Description: A heavily bodied fish with brown/olive background coloring overlaid with numerous darker blotches. There is a distinct dark blotch where the lateral line meets the caudal fin. Mature fish have bright turquoise coloring over the belly, breast and cheeks. Eyes are red.

Size: Seldom exceed 12 inches; most are less than 1 pound in weight.

IGFA All-Tackle World Record 3 pound 14 ounces, Suwannee River, FL, USA.

Tackle and fishing: A very strong fighter for its size. Most are caught when anglers are targeting other species. They are best targeted using very light spin, baitcasting or fly fishing tackle. Popular rigs include crankbaits, plastic worms, jigs, in-line spinners and plugs. Natural baits such as small minnows, worms and crawfish are all popular.

Edibility: Excellent.

Game status: Very good. On very light tackle.

BASS, WHITE

Scientific name: Morone chrysops. Also known as silver bass, sand bass, barfish, streaker.

Range: Large reservoirs, natural lakes and large rivers throughout the east, southeast mid and southwest. Not restricted to its natural range due to transplanting and now available over wide areas.

Habitat: Adult fish are usually found in schools and feed near the surface on emerging insects or schools of baitfish. Often around areas such as points and promontories that create runs and eddies that funnel food items, or when spontaneous surface attacks occur on baitfish schools. Fish often concentrate in spring below dams.

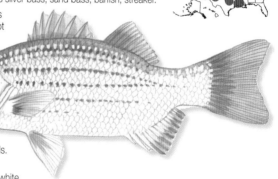

Description: Dark gray/black on back with a silver white coloring on flanks and belly. Several broken and incomplete longitudinal lines or stripes along the sides that can confuse anglers into thinking these fish are small striped bass. One way of distinguishing the fish is by the gill plate spines. Striped bass have two points whereas white bass have one.

Size: Normally ranges between 1 and 2 pound. Maximum size around 7 pound.

IGFA All-Tackle World Record 6 pound 13 ounces, Lake Orange, VA, USA.

Tackle and fishing: Excellent fighting fish for their size, and especially so when taken on light tackle. When schools are located, good fishing can be had using spoons, spinners, crankbaits and jigs as well as top water or diving plugs on spin and baitcasting outfits. Popping bugs and streamer flies are successful, as is baitfishing with live minnows. Bottom fishing with live baits after dark is also worthwhile.

Edibility: Good.

Game status: Good.

BASS, YELLOW

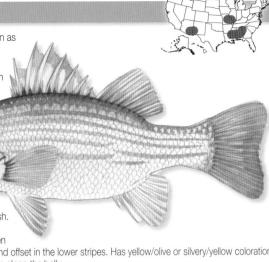

Scientific name: Morone mississppiensis. Also known as barfish, streaker, brassy bass, striper.

Range: Native to the south and Midwestern United States. Found in the Mississippi River drainage after which it was named. Introduced populations occur in Arizona, Iowa, Wisconsin and Tennessee.

Habitat: Throughout large streams and lakes of the drainage. Natural lakes, reservoirs and large river backwaters. It has a preference for clear to slightly colored waters over a firm bottom substrate of gravel, sand, rock and mud. Often found in schools.

Description: A laterally compressed and slab sided fish. Sometimes confused with white bass and striped bass, although distinguished by its yellow belly and six or seven dark horizontal stripes along the body that are broken and offset in the lower stripes. Has yellow/olive or silvery/yellow coloration along the back and sides that fade to lighter yellow/white along the belly.

Size: Average length of yellow bass is 11 inches, and half a pound or less in weight. Maximum size around 3 pounds.

IGFA All-Tackle World Record 2 pound 9 ounces, Duck River, TN, USA

Tackle and fishing: Tough fighters despite their size. Can be caught on spin, fly and baitcasting tackle and will take plugs and natural baits. They feed at mid water or near the surface during low light periods of the day.

Edibility: Excellent.

Game status: Good. When taken on appropriate tackle.

BLACKFISH, SACRAMENTO

Scientific name: Orthodon microlepidotus.

Range: Native to the Sacramento River and San Joaquin River drainages. Also in Clear Lake. Other streams and lakes in California and Nevada.

Habitat: Prefer warm turbid waters in small to large streams. Mostly plankton feeders.

Description: Elongated round body covered in tiny scales. They have a thin caudal peduncle, a flat sloping head and small eyes. Upturned and thin lips.

Coloring in adult fish is light to dark gray with an olive sheen. Fins are gray.

Size: Most are less than 10 inches. Rarely exceed 20 inches and 3 pounds.

Tackle and fishing: Not a bad fighter but rarely targeted or hooked due to its feeding habits. Will take baits such as worms, dough and corn fished on or near the bottom using poles and spin tackle.

Edibility: Good.

Game status: Fair. Rarely caught.

BLUEGILL

Scientific name: Lepomismacrochirus. Also known as bream, brim, perch, blue bream, sunfish, sunpearch, blue sunfish, sunny.

Range: Native to the eastern half of the United States, northeastern Mexico and southeastern Canada.

Due to extensive stocking and transplanting, they are now widespread throughout the United States, including Hawaii, and northern Mexico.

Habitat: Throughout ponds, rivers and lakes.

They often overpopulate waters due to their long spawning season and fertile reproduction rates.

They often hang about structure such as lillypads and move into shallow water (1-2 feet deep), over gravel when spawning.

Description: Distinguished from other sunfish by the dark spot at the base of the dorsal fin, dark vertical bars along the flanks and the pronounced solid black/blue flap at eth rear edge of the gill cover.

Coloring is generally dark olive/green dorsally blending to a copper brown, lavender and orange along the sides. The breast area is yellow or orange/red, which is most prominent in breeding fish.

Size: Can reach 4 pounds. Most fish are more likely between 8 -12 ounces in weight.

IGFA All-Tackle World Record 4 pound 12 ounces, Ketona Lake, AL, USA.

Tackle and fishing: Lots of anglers 'cut their teeth' catching bluegill and other sunfish. They are scrappy fighters and good fun when caught on light tackle such as spin, fly and fishing poles. They willingly hit small lures, spinners, poppers, jigs and small wet flies and nymphs as well as natural baits such as meal worms, freshwater shrimp, crickets, small baitfish plus corn kernels, bacon and bread dough.

Edibility: Very good. Flavour is dependant on the water quality from where the fish was caught. Skinning fish can help flavour.

Game status: Excellent. Not a great fighter but very popular target species.

BONYTAIL

Scientific name: Gila elegans. Also known as bonytail chub.

Range: Colorado River of Arizona, California, Colorado, Utah and Nevada.

Endangered in many areas within its range due to habitat alterations and predation by non-native fish species.

Habitat: Prefer river backwaters and flowing pools over rocky or mud bottoms.

Description: A streamlined body with a noticeable hump behind the head in adult fish. The caudal peduncle is long and thin. Coloration is dark blue/brown or gray/black above and lighter on the flanks and belly. Breeding males have bright orange/red lateral bands between their pectoral fins.

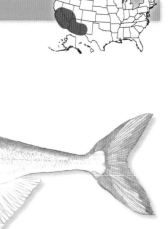

Size: Can grow to over 24 inches in length.

Tackle and fishing: Not recognised for its fighting abilities. Most are taken by accident when anglers are chasing other fish using baits such as worms.

Edibility: N/A. Should be released and not targeted.

Game status: N/A. Should be released and not targeted.

BOWFIN

Scientific name: Amia calva. Also known as blackfish, mudfish, grindle, dogfish, cypress trout.

Range: Eastern United States (not in the Appalachians) from the Great Lakes to the Gulf of Mexico. They inhabit the drainage basins of Lake Superior, Lake Michigan and the Mississippi River.

Habitat: Prefer warm, low oxygenated waters. Swamps and lowland streams. Around the edges of aquatic vegetation. Often seen gulping air in stagnant water such as ponds.

Description: Bowfin can survive for out of the water for a considerable length of time. They have an air bladder that acts as a lung, allowing them to gulp air from the surface as well as breathing underwater. A long, stout, cylindrical body with a long dorsal fin and rounded caudal fin. A big mouth with small sharp teeth. These fish are slippery and anglers should avoid being bitten. Male fish have a dark spot haloed by orange in front of the caudal fin. This spot is absent in female bowfin. Color is dark brown/ olive/yellowish with darker twirls and patterning along the back and flanks.

Size: Can grow to 19 pounds in weight but mostly caught between 2-8 pounds.

IGFA All-Tackle World Record 21 pound 8 ounces, Florence, SC, USA.

Tackle and fishing: Despite its less than agile appearance, the bowfin is a tough fighter. They are a stalking, ambush feeding fish. They are an aggressive fish that will hit a variety of lures, on the surface or below, and eat just about any type of bait, live, dead or cut. Usually caught on spin and baitcasting outfits.

Edibility: Poor. Rarely eaten. Flesh is not firm.

Game status: Very good.

BUFFALO, BIGMOUTH

Scientific name: Ictiobus cyprinellus. Also known as redmouth buffalo, buffalo fish, buffalo sucker, Bernard buffalo, roundhead, brown buffalo, gourd head.

Range: From Manitoba, Canada to the Mississippi River system in Texas and Alabama.

Habitat: Sluggish waters in large rivers, shallow lakes and streams. Prefers areas with aquatic vegetation and soft bottoms.

Description: Dull brown/olive above with dusky colored fins. Sides are yellow/copper tinged and belly is pale yellow/ white.

A heavy bodied, large headed fish with heavy 'buffalo' shaped shoulders and one long dorsal fin. There are no barbels on the mouth or spines on fins. Similar in general appearance to the common carp.

Size: The largest of the buffalo fish. Can grow to 4 feet and weigh 65 pounds. Most average between 2-10 pounds, but it's not uncommon to see fish of twice this size.

IGFA All-Tackle World Record 70 pound 5 ounces, Bussey Brake, Bastrop, LA, USA.

Tackle and fishing: A solid fighter that is rarely taken with rod and line, but those that are will test any anglers tackle, especially bigger fish. Strong spin and baitcasting tackle using bottom baits such as worms or dough on small hooks. Sometimes taken with trotlines and by anglers spearing fish or using bows.

Edibility: Good. Numerous small bones.

Game status: Very good.

BUFFALO, BLACK

Scientific name: Ictiobus niger. Also known as lake buffalo, round buffalo.

Range: Canada to the Mississippi. Missouri and Ohio. Lower Great lakes states to the plains states. Introduced elsewhere. Not common like other buffalos.

Habitat: Pools, eddies and backwaters of small to large rivers. Shallow vegetated areas of lakes and impoundments. Threatened in areas due to habitat alteration.

Description: A large sucker fish that is gray/olive/bronze on the back with a blue and olive iridescence. Olive/yellow sides and white/yellow belly. Fins are olive/black. A large conical head with a sucker-type mouth. Similar in general appearance to common carp.

Size: Can grow to 37 inches. Most would average 2-10 pounds. Can grow to over 50 pounds in weight.

IGFA All-Tackle World Record 63 pound 3 ounces, Mississippi River, IA, USA.

Tackle and fishing: A very strong fish that requires stout spin or baitcasting tackle to subdue. Worms, dough and corn baits are successful.

Edibility: Very good.

Game status: Very good.

BUFFALO, SMALLMOUTH

Scientific name: Micropterus dolomieu. Also known as smallmouth, brown bass, bronzeback, smallie, bronze bass.

Range: Native to the Hudson Bay basin, Saint Lawrence River system and the upper and middle Mississippi River basin. Heavily transplanted and now in all states except Alaska, Louisiana and Florida.

Habitat: Prefers cooler water temperatures than Largemouth bass. It also prefers clearer (flowing) waters of streams and rivers and prefers sandy (less weedy areas) lakebeds, especially around rock and submerged tree structure.

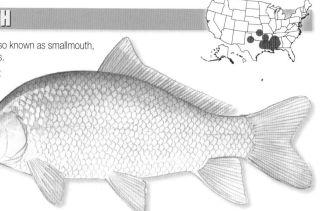

They prefer clean, unpolluted water.

Description: Mostly brown (bronze) dorsally with paler brown/greenish flanks overlaid with dark vertical bands. Belly is pale yellow/white. The upper jaw only extends back to be in line with the middle of the eye.

The habitat in which they live usually influences their coloration.

Size: Most fish taken average around 1-2 pounds. Fish of twice this weight aren't rare. Male fish are generally smaller than females.

IGFA All-Tackle World Record 10 pound 14 ounces, Dale hollow, TN, USA.

Tackle and fishing: A very good (one of the best) fighting fish that is both strong and acrobatic. Because they tend to prefer open water areas they can be targeted using lighter tackle that also allows them to put up a better fight. They eat various foods including frogs, insects, crayfish and even small mice.

They are usually fished for with light spin and baitcasting tackle as well as fly tackle where appropriate. They can be caught on a range of natural and artificial baits and lures. Jigs, crankbaits, spinnerbaits, plastic jerkbaits are all productive as are various wet and dry flies.

Natural baits as mentioned above are all successful.

Edibility: Excellent. Fillets are white and firm when cooked. Most fish are released however.

Game status: Excellent. The best of all the freshwater bass.

BULLHEAD, BLACK

Scientific name: Ameiurus melas. Also known as mudcat, polliwog, chucklehead cat, horned pout.

Range: Throughout central United States.

Habitat: Generally in slow moving or stagnant waters with soft bottoms. Extremely tolerant to warm, muddy water with low oxygen levels. It is a bottom dwelling fish.

Description: Like most bullheads it has a squared tail. A slightly humped back. Color often dependent on the water in which it lives, but mostly black, dark brown or dusky gray/green on back and sides with a yellow or white belly area. The lower lip does not protrude past the upper lip. Chin barbels are always dark or black, never white.

Size: Generally 1-2 pounds, rarely more than 5 pounds. Most fish are 8-15 inches in length.

IGFA All-Tackle World Record 7 pound 7 ounces, Mill Pond, NY, USA.

Tackle and fishing: Not a great fighter. Usually taken with poles or light spincasting tackle using small natural baits such as worms, or food items such as cheese, corn or dough.

Edibility: Very good.

Game status: Fair. Mostly too small.

BULLHEAD, BROWN

Scientific name: Ameiurusnebulosus. Also known as brown catfish, squaretail cat, mud pout, horned pout, mud cat.

Range: Eastern North America. Nova Scotia to Florida. Transplanted widely elsewhere.

Habitat: Warm, slow-flowing rivers, streams, ponds, lakes and reservoirs. They will tolerate areas of high water pollution. Shallow areas predominantly, but down to 40 feet over soft bottoms with lots of vegetation. Primarily a bottom swimming, night feeder.

Description: A square shaped tail, a brown/black colored nose,chin and upper lip barbels. Body coloring is darker brown/black dorsally fading to a lighter brown with distinctive irregular darker brown mottling below. Belly area is creamy white.

Size: Can grow to 6 pounds. Most catches are less than one pound in weight. Not uncommon at 16 inches in length and two pound in weight.

IGFA All-Tackle World Record 6 pound 1 ounce, Waterford, NY, USA.

Tackle and fishing: Offer a reasonable fight on light tackle. Most anglers use poles or spin tackle. They will take baits such as worms, shrimp and minnows. Also stinkbaits, cheese, bread dough and chicken liver. Although they are night feeders, anglers do catch them throughout the day.

Edibility: Very good. Delicious when caught in clearwater.

Game status: Good.

BULLHEAD, SNAIL CONTINUED...

Scientific name: Ameiurus brunneus. Also known as mudcat.

Range: Common in much of its range. Northern Georgia, northern Florida.

Habitat: Swift flowing streams in rocky riffles, pools and runs.

Description: A very rounded snout and flat head. Coloration is yellow/brown olive above and blue/white or white below. Some have a mottled appearance while others not so. A large dark blotch at the base of the dorsal fin. The tail is square shaped and tipped in black.

Size: A small fish that grows to 11.5 inches in length. Usually less than half a pound in weight.

Tackle and fishing: Too small to offer much in the way sport. Usually taken with poles or very light spin tackle using small natural baits or food such as dough, corn or cheese.

Edibility: Excellent.

Game status: N/A. Too small.

BULLHEAD, SPOTTED

Scientific name: Ameiurus serracanthus. Also known as speckled cat.

Range: An uncommon fish that lives in streams on the Gulf coastal plains of northern Florida, south-eastern Alabama and southern Georgia.

Habitat: Small to medium rivers with swift currents in deep rock or sand filled pools. Also shallow ponds and impoundments.

Description: Coloration is dark blue/black above with golden sheen. Lighter below, and with a white belly. The body is covered with light gray/white spots. The fins are edged in black and there is a large dark blotch at the base of the dorsal fin. It is the only North American catfish with light round spots over a dark colored body.

Size: Rarely longer than 11 inches in length.

Tackle and fishing: Its diminutive size restricts any fighting abilities. Usually taken with poles or light spincasting gear using worms, small minnows, cheese, and dough.

Edibility: Excellent.

Game status: N/A. Too small

BULLHEAD, YELLOW

Scientific name: Ameiurus natalis. Also known as butter cat, butter ball, mudcat, polliwog, chucklehead cat.

Range: Throughout central and eastern United States from central Texas to North Dakota and the Great Lakes region to the coast. Widely transplanted elsewhere.

Habitat: A bottom dweller that prefers pools with silt/mud bottoms in small to medium sized rivers. Can be found in a variety of different habitats including well-vegetated ponds and lakes.

BULLHEAD, YELLOW CONTINUED...

Description: Typically olive green/brown or yellow above (sometimes mottled) with yellow sides and yellow or white belly. The tail is square with rounded tips. A long anal fin. The chin barbels are white.

Size: Usually 6-10 inches and less than 1 pound. Can grow to twice this or more at times.

IGFA All-Time World Record 4 pound 4 ounces, Mormon Lake, AZ, USA.

Tackle and fishing: Easily caught with poles and light spincasting tackle using worms, cut baits, crickets, doughballs, cheese, corn and prepared baits.

Edibility: Very good.

Game status: Average. Mostly too small.

BURDOT

Scientific name: Lota lota. Also known as ling, the lawyer, bubbot, freshwater ling, Mariah.

Range: Very widespread. Alaska to New Brunswick along the Atlantic Coast. Great Lakes.

Habitat: Streams and lakes. Often very deep, but moving into shallower waters in spring.

Description: A serpentine like, slender body. Elongated and compressed with a flattened head, wide mouth with numerous small teeth and single barbell on the chin. Two dorsal fins with the rear fin being long. The anal fin is also long. Coloration is mottled dark brown dorsally fading to lighter mottled brown below and cream belly.

Size: Most are between 10-20 inches in length. Can grow 25 pounds.

IGFA All-Tackle World Record 18 pound 11 ounces, Angenmanelren, Sweden.

Tackle and fishing: Certainly no fighter with those fins. A tenacious predator that will eat lures and baits intended for other fish such as lake trout. Mostly caught when fishing deep, often when ice-fishing using jigs, spoons and baits.

Considered a real threat to trout fisheries in some areas due to their habit of feeding on trout and salmon eggs.

Edibility: Good.

Game status: Poor.

CARP, BIGHEAD

Scientific name: Hypophthalmichthys nobilis. Also known as Chinese carp, bigmouth carp.

Range: A native fish of Asia. Accidentally introduced into the Mississippi River basin and is considered a highly invasive and destructive species. Spread into some other areas.

Habitat: A filter feeder. Often found schooling with paddlefish.

Description: A large head that has no scales, a large mouth, and eyes located very low on the head. Coloring is mostly a mottled silver/gray/olive with paler lower sides and belly.

Size: Average size 24-30 inches but can grow to around 100 pounds.

IGFA All-Tackle World Record 61 pound 15 ounces, Old Hickory Lake, TN, USA.

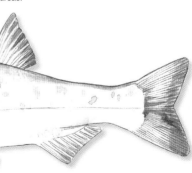

Tackle and fishing: Very rarely captured on baited hooks because of their feeding habits. When they are hooked with rod and line they put up a solid fight. A very popular bowfishing target because they swim close to the surface. Fish are often jagged with weighted treble hooks.

Edibility: Good. Not popular in the U.S.

Game status: Very good. Rarely hooked.

CARP, COMMON

Scientific name: Cyprinus carpio. Also known as German carp, European carp.

Range: One of the most widely distributed fish in North America, from central Canada to central Mexico. Distributed through intentional and unintentional liberations.

Habitat: Almost any and every freshwater habitat. Lakes, channels, rivers and ponds, and clear or turbid water conditions. Probably have a preference for slow waters and ponds with good aquatic vegetation.

Description: A heavy bodied fish with barbells on each side of the lower jaw. Color varies from brassy yellow or green, to golden brown. The belly is mostly yellow/white. Fins often have a reddish tinge.

Size: Commonly from 12-25 inches in length and between 8-10 pounds in weight. They can grow much larger. Have been known to reach 75 pounds in weight.

IGFA All-Tackle World Record 75 pound 11 ounces, St.Cassien, France.

Tackle and fishing: Generally regarded as a nuisance fish by many anglers. They have a reputation for destroying the water environment for other preferred or native fish. Their fighting ability is extremely good; they are strong and solid fighters. They are slowly gaining favour with anglers because of their fighting prowess and because they are so abundant and grow so big in many areas.

They can be caught using spin, baitcasting and fly tackle. Most are caught on natural baits such as worms. They will eat dough balls, corn kernels and cheese and hit very small lures and wet flies.

Edibility: Poor. Flavour varies in quality.

Game status: Excellent.

CARP, GRASS

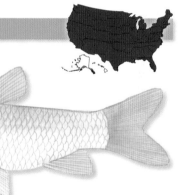

Scientific name: Ctenopharyngodon idella. Also known as white amur.

Range: A native fish of eastern Asia. Introduced into the United States to control aquatic weed upon which it feeds. Throughout major river systems in the United States.

Habitat: Occurs in lakes, ponds, pools and backwaters of large rivers where there is low or no flow and abundant aquatic vegetation.

Description: An elongated body. Lips aren't fleshy and there ate no barbels around the mouth. Coloration is dark olive/brown on the back, with brown/gold/yellow flanks and white belly.

Size: A fast growing fish that averages 24-39 inches in length and 5-15 pounds in weigh. They can grow to 4' 6" inches and 88 pounds.

Tackle and fishing: Strong fighters once hooked. They aren't easily taken with baits because they are mostly weed eaters. Chumming with corn and bread will often result in fish taking a baited hook of dough, bread, corn or similar. They are mostly targeted with spin, bait or flycasting tackle. They are a popular bowfishing species where legal.

Edibility: Poor.

Game status: Excellent. Hard to deceive and a good fighter.

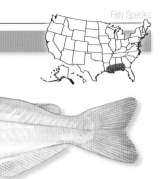

CATFISH, BLUE

Scientific name: Ictalurus furcatus. Also known as silver catfish, channel cat, humpback blue.

Range: Native to the major rivers of the Ohio, Mississippi and Missouri river basins. Into Mexico, and introduced into many rivers along the Atlantic Coast.

Habitat: Blue Catfish inhabit large rivers, the main channels and tributaries and lakes of the major rivers. They prefer reasonably clear and flowing water. They often move about in search of cooler water in summer and warmer water in winter.

They frequent deep holes in flowing water, often around current edges and breaks.

Description: An elongated body. Lips aren't fleshy and there ate no barbels around the mouth. Coloration is dark olive/brown on the back, with brown/gold/yellow flanks and white belly.

Size: Commonly grow to 20-40 pounds. Many reach 100 pounds.

IGFA All-Tackle World Record 116 pound 12 ounces, Mississippi River, AR, USA.

Tackle and fishing: The largest of all the catfish. Its size alone equates to a serious tussle, even on heavy tackle, but even 'smaller' fish are solid fighters. Trotliners often catch the largest fish. Heavy spin, baitcasting or even light saltwater tackle is not out of place when tackling these big fish. They will take numerous baits including live (or dead) fish such as herring and shad, large cut baits, pieces of meat, crayfish and prepared baits.

Edibility: Excellent.

Game status: Excellent. One of the most popular fish for southern anglers.

CATFISH, CHANNEL

Scientific name: Ictalurus punctatus. Also known as speckled cat, river cat, willow cat, fiddler, forked-tail cat, spotted cat, lady cat.

Range: Native to North America, east of the Rockies from southern Canada and south into northeastern Mexico. Now widely introduced as far west as California and also Hawaii.

Habitat: Most abundant in slow or moderate flowing large streams. Usually in deep holes throughout the daylight hours. Also in lakes, especially around inflowing streams. They prefer warm water averaging 70 degrees Fahrenheit.

Description: Best identified by their deeply forked tail fin. Coloring is mostly olive brown to pale slate gray, or light blue/gray on the back and sides. White or yellowish along the belly. There are often numerous small black spots along the flanks, which are most obvious on smaller fish. Upper jaw projects past the lower jaw. Eyes are small. They have eight barbels around the mouth, four of which are on the chin.

Can be mistaken for blue catfish (Ictalurus furcatus)

Size: Generally between 15-24 inches in length. Most common to 4 pounds. Bigger fish aren't uncommon and it can grow to over 50 pounds.

IGFA All-Tackle World Record 58 pound, Santee-Cooper Res. SC, USA.

Tackle and fishing: A very popular fish that gives a good account of itself when hooked. Will take artificial lures but is rarely deliberately targeted with anything other than baits. Usually caught using heavier spin and baitcasting outfits for bigger fish and lighter outfits and poles for small specimens. Popular with trotliners where legal.

They will take most baits. Live and dead baitfish, crawfish, cut baits, worms, dough balls, liver, chicken innards, cheese, crickets, grasshoppers and stinkbaits.

Also 'noodled', a method where the fish is caught by hand. States where this practice is presently legal are Mississippi, Alabama, Arkansas, North Carolina, Missouri and Georgia.

Edibility: Excellent. A delicious eating fish.

Game status: Good.

CATFISH, FLATHEAD

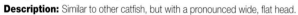

Scientific name: Also known as mudcat, yellow cat, Apaloosa cat, shovelhead catfish, Mississippi cat, pied cat, Opelousa cat.

Range: Lower Great Lakes through the Mississippi River drainage to the Gulf States. Widely transplanted into various areas.

Habitat: Deep slow pools in streams, canals, rivers, reservoirs and lakes. They prefer turbid water conditions. Usually a solitary fish once they attain any size.

Description: Similar to other catfish, but with a pronounced wide, flat head. Smooth skin with barbels around mouth and long sharp spines on the dorsal fin. Coloring is pale yellow to light brown on the back and sides overlaid with dark brown or blackish mottling. Belly area is cream or white. The tail is square but slightly notched and the tip of the upper lobe is cream/white. Juveniles are often almost black in color.

Size: Can reach 3-4 feet in length and 100 pounds in weight. Common between 15-30 pounds. Most fish caught are probably half those weights.

IGFA All-Tackle World Record 123 pounds, Elk City Res. KS, USA.

Tackle and fishing: Unlike other catfish, once this species reaches approximately 10-12 inches it starts to feed exclusively on live fish. They are strong, if not flashy fighters. The big specimens require stout rods and gear to subdue them. Smaller fish can be taken on lighter spin and baitcast tackle, or poles. Anglers using trotlines traditionally catch the biggest fish. Rod and line anglers often do very well immediately below reservoir walls.

Live fish are by far the best baits for the bigger fish. Smaller fish will take various baits such as worms and manufactured 'kitchen' baits. In some areas 'noodling', or catching catfish with bare hands is popular.

Edibility: Excellent.

Game status: Very good. Not spectacular though.

CATFISH, WALKING

Scientific name: Clarias batrachus.

Range: A non-native (Asia) population was established in southern Florida and other areas often due to the release of private aquarium fish.

Habitat: A wide variety of habitats including rivers and lakes. Usual habitat consists of warm stagnant water in ponds, canals, ditches and swamp areas. They are best known for their ability to survive where other fish can't as well as move about over land and breath air.

Description: All over gray or gray/brown coloring with numerous small white spots along the body. The head is flat and wide and the body tapers towards the tail. Very small eyes, lengthy dorsal and anal fins. Unlike North American catfish it does not have an adipose fin.

The walking catfish moves about on land with the aid of its stiff pectoral fins and a side-to-side body flexing motion.

Size: Can grow to 24 inches. North American fish to 14 inches in length.

Tackle and fishing: Sometimes taken with worms and other panfish baits by accident.

Edibility: N/A. Valued food source in Asia.

Game status: N/A.

CATFISH, WHITE

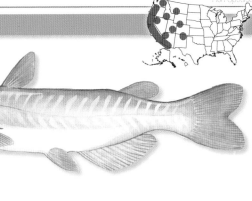

Scientific name: Clarias batrachus.

Also known as white bullhead, forked-tailed cat.

Range: A non-native (Asia) population was established in southern Florida and other areas often due to the release of private aquarium fish.

Habitat: A wide variety of habitats including rivers and lakes. Usual habitat consists of warm stagnant water in ponds, canals, ditches and swamp areas. They are best known for their ability to survive where other fish can't as well as move about over land and breath air.

Description: All over gray or gray/brown coloring with numerous small white spots along the body. The head is flat and wide and the body tapers towards the tail. Very small eyes, lengthy dorsal and anal fins. Unlike North American catfish it does not have an adipose fin.

The walking catfish moves about on land with the aid of its stiff pectoral fins and a side-to-side body flexing motion.

Size: Can grow to 24 inches. North American fish to 14 inches in length.

Tackle and fishing: Sometimes taken with worms and other panfish baits by accident.

Edibility: N/A. Valued food source in Asia.

Game status: N/A.

CHAR, ARCTIC

Scientific name: Salvelinus alpinus. Three species exist in North America. Also known as Blueback char.

Range: Ranges from Northern Quebec, Newfoundland to Baffin Island on the Atlantic (east) Coast. Arctic and sub-Arctic, Alaska and Canada and some landlocked New England waters.

Habitat: Once in freshwater fish will hang about feeding in stream riffles and school up in deep river pools and deep lake areas.

Sea-run fish inhabit river mouths and estuaries.

Description: Freshwater fish tend to be highly variable in colour depending on their environment, especially lake fish. They tend to be green or brown above with pink/orange or deep red below. Females tend to remain duller and silvery while spawning males display very vivid colours with white or red dots along the flanks if these are present. There are no markings on the dorsal or tail fins.

Flesh can be bright red or pale pink.

Size: Generally 2-5 pounds. Bigger fish aren't uncommon, especially in areas where fresh run fish are present.

IGFA All-Tackle World Record 32 pound 9 ounces, Tree River, Canada.

Tackle and fishing: Hard fighters but not as lively or strong as the sea runners or fresh from salt fish. As they migrate upstream to spawn their condition and fighting abilities deteriorate. Arctic char predominantly feed on small baitfish so spin of baitcasting shiny spoons, spinners or swimming minnow's accounts for most fish. They will willingly hit fish imitating streamer flies in rivers and lakes and occasionally take dry flies when the fish are feeding on surface insects. Lake fish will take other attractor wet flies or nymphs also.

Edibility: Very good. When fish are fresh-run or landlocked. Spawning fish are less appetising.

Game status: Excellent. Landlocked or fresh run fish. Less so as spawning fish move further upstream.

CHUB, LAKE

Scientific name: Couesius plumbeus. Also known as northern chub, chub minnow, lake northern chub, bottlefish.

Range: Throughout Canada. Arctic Circle. Great Lakes region, plus New England, Iowa, Michigan, Wisconsin, Montana, Colorado, Wyoming, Washington, Idaho and Utah. The northern most North American minnows.

Habitat: Most commonly found in lakes where they frequent rocky shorelines. They move into deeper water to avoid warmer summer temperatures. They travel out of lakes and into streams to spawn. Lower elevation slow flowing streams.

Description: Overall silver/gray with dusky olive/brown or darker brown back and white belly. An indistinct midline darker band running from the snout to the start of the tail fin. Splattering of dark scales can give speckled appearance and breeding males develop orange/red patches at the base of their pectoral fins and sometimes near their mouth. A barbell is located just above each corner of the mouth.

Size: Average around 4 inches but can grow to around 8-10 inches.

Tackle and fishing: A scrappy little fighter when caught on light fly or spin tackle. Also taken using poles. Most are caught on small baits.

Edibility: Fair. Bony.

Game status: Fair. Usually too small.

CHUB, CREEK

Scientific name: Semotilus atromaculatus.

Range: Throughout eastern United States and south eastern Canada.

Habitat: Most abundant in small streams in rocky and sandy pools. Often in tiny headwater areas. They can tolerate a wide variety of water conditions.

Description: A thick bodied fish with a broad head and large mouth. The upper jaw extends beyond the front of the eye. Coloration is olive/brown dorsally with a dark stripe that runs the full length of the body and a dark spot on the front edge of the dorsal fin where it meets the body. Large breeding males have an orange/red color on their cheeks, lips, belly and lower fins.

Size: From 4-8 inches in length but can reach 12 inches.

Tackle and fishing: Not large enough to offer any resistance. Anglers chasing them for bait using nets take most of these fish. Can also be caught using poles and dough or worm baits, or by flyfishers targeting trout with wet flies.

Edibility: Poor.

Game status: Poor. Targeted for use as bait for larger sportfish.

CHUB, DIXIE

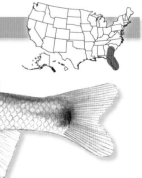

Scientific name: Semotilus thoreauianus.

Range: Gulf slope drainages from the Mobile basin east to the Ochlockonee river drainage in Georgia and Florida.

Habitat: Headwater streams with riffles and pools over sand/gravel substrates.

Description: Body resembles that of the Creek Chub. Have a more robust body with a

CHUB, DIXIE CONTINUED...

wider and a less prominent strip along the flanks. Darker olive/brown/black above with whitish underside. Breeding males have orange/pink undersides with yellow fins.

Size: Can grow to around 6 inches.

Tackle and fishing: Not targeted with sport fishing tackle. Usually sought for use as bait using nets or poles. Best bait is small pieces of earthworm.

Edibility: N/A.

Game status: N/A. Used as bait.

CHUB, HORNYHEAD

Scientific name: Semotilus thoreauianus. Also known as white bullhead, forked-tailed cat.

Range: Gulf slope drainages from the Mobile basin east to the Ochlockonee river drainage in Georgia and Florida.

Habitat: Headwater streams with riffles and pools over sand/gravel substrates.

Description: Body resembles that of the Creek Chub. Have a more robust body with a wider and a less prominent strip along the flanks. Darker olive/brown/black above with whitish underside. Breeding males have orange/pink undersides with yellow fins.

Size: Can grow to around 6 inches.

Tackle and fishing: Not targeted with sport fishing tackle. Usually sought for use as bait using nets or poles. Best bait is small pieces of earthworm.

Edibility: N/A.

Game status: N/A. Used as bait.

CHUB, HUMPBACK

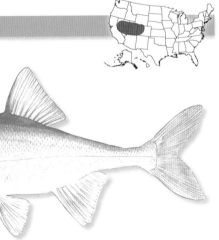

Scientific name: Gila cypha.

Range: Colorado and Green Rivers in Colorado, Wyoming, Utah and Arizona. Altered habitat due to dams has had an adverse effect on populations as had predation by non-native fish.

Habitat: High volume, canyon bound areas of the Colorado River basin. As fish increase in size and age they move into faster and deeper water.

Description: A streamlined fish with a pronounced hump immediately behind the head, and a very long, thin caudal peduncle leading to a deeply forked tail. Small eyes, and a protruding fleshy snout. The body has no scales and is light olive gray above, with silver sides and a white belly.

Size: Mostly between 5-6 inches in length. Can grow to 15-19 inches.

Tackle and fishing: Not targeted by recreational anglers. Most are caught by accident by anglers fishing with wet flies or worm baits.

Edibility: N/A.

Game status: N/A.

CHUB, ROUNDTAIL

Scientific name: Gila robusta.

Range: Colorado River drainage basin from the headwaters to the mouth. In Colorado, Arizona, Nevada, Utah, California and north west Mexico.

Habitat: Prefers moderate sized rivers where it occupies pools and eddies, often in water immediately below rapids. Common in a number of western lakes.

Description: A deep, streamlined body with dark olive/gray/ brown back and silver flanks. A large, deeply forked tail. Breeding males develop orange/red coloration on the lower cheek and at the base of the pectoral fins.

Size: Between 8-18 inches in length and to over 3 pounds in weight.

Tackle and fishing: A solid and respected sportfish that puts up a good fight on lighter tackle. Will take similar lures, flies and baits as trout. Caught on fly and spin tackle as well as poles using worms, crickets, minnows, small spinners and spoons and wet flies.

Edibility: Fair. Firm and white flesh but bony.

Game status: Very good.

CHUBSUCKER, CREEK

Scientific name: Erimyson oblongus.

Range: Great Lakes to the Mississippi drainage in the Gulf. Eastern coastal plains and in mid-western streams east of the Central Plains.

Habitat: Clear headwater creeks in vegetated runs, pools and riffles.

Description: A small chubsucker with a dark golden/ bronze back and upper sides with a cream/white belly. The scale edges are marked in black, which give the fish a cross-hatched appearance over the body. There are a row of 5-8 faint saddles along the back and upper sides and a row of blotches along the mid flanks that give the appearance of a broad stripe.

Size: Typically 4-6 inches in length, but can reach 8 inches.

Tackle and fishing: Taken with poles using small pieces of bait such as worm, crayfish and aquatic insects.

Edibility: N/A.

Game status: N/A.

CHUBSUCKER, LAKE

Scientific name: Erimyzon sucetta.

Range: Great Lakes and Mississippi River basin lowlands. Texas and across the southeast from Louisiana to Virginia.

Populations are declining in areas due to habitat modification, invasive species and pollution.

Habitat: Warm clear Stillwater areas with low turbidity. Mostly across wetlands, floodplain lakes and ponds. Prefers shallow areas.

Description: A medium sized fish with a stubby body, large scales, blunt snout and small eyes. Coloration of adult fish is similar to the creek chubsucker

CHUBSUCKER, LAKE CONTINUED...

but lacking the blotches along the sides. They are dark olive/green above with silver/gold sides and a green/yellow belly area. Young fish have a prominent dark stripe along the flanks that disappears with age.

Size: Grow to 8-10 inches.

Tackle and fishing: Too small to offer any real fight. Most are caught on light spin tackle and worm or aquatic insect baits.

Edibility: Poor.

Game status: Poor.

CICHLID, MAYAN

Scientific name: Erimyzon sucetta.

Range: Great Lakes and Mississippi River basin lowlands. Texas and across the southeast from Louisiana to Virginia.

Populations are declining in areas due to habitat modification, invasive species and pollution.

Habitat: Warm clear Stillwater areas with low turbidity. Mostly across wetlands, floodplain lakes and ponds. Prefers shallow areas.

Description: A medium sized fish with a stubby body, large scales, blunt snout and small eyes. Coloration of adult fish is similar to the creek chubsucker but lacking the blotches along the sides. They are dark olive/green above with silver/gold sides and a green/yellow belly area. Young fish have a prominent dark stripe along the flanks that disappears with age.

Size: Grow to 8-10 inches.

Tackle and fishing: Too small to offer any real fight. Most are caught on light spin tackle and worm or aquatic insect baits.

Edibility: Poor.

Game status: Poor.

CICHLID, MIDAS

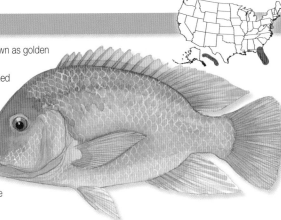

Scientific name: Cichlasoma citrinellum. Also known as golden cichlid.

Range: Native fish of Tropical America. Now established in Hawaii, Florida, occasionally elsewhere. Most introductions are from aquarium or fish farm releases.

Habitat: Mostly vegetated areas along canals. Often near submerged structure.

Description: A heavily built fish with powerful jaws and sharp teeth. Color varies greatly with most being gray to olive brown with black bars. Others can be pink, white, and yellow. Often fish are golden yellow/orange with faint/white or darker bars and markings.

Size: Mostly very small.

Tackle and fishing: Usually taken with poles or ultra light spin tackle using dough, worms. Very occasionally on small flies and spinners.

Edibility: Good.

Game status: N/A.

CICHLID, PEACOCK

Scientific name: Cichla ocellaris. Also known as peacock bass, butterfly bass.

Range: A native to South America. It has been introduced into the United States, mostly Hawaii and Florida. Its intolerance to cooler water temperatures restricts its ability to be introduced elsewhere.

Habitat: Mostly close to the edges, around structure and vegetated areas in canals and lakes, mostly in residential areas.

Description: Similar body shape to bass. A visually striking fish. Peacock bass are brightly colored with the main body area being yellow or gold with a white belly. The dorsal fin is black and the tail fin is black above and yellow/orange below. They have three or four vertical dark bars that don't extend past the lateral line. They have a row of broken darker splotches running horizontally from behind the gill plate to the tail and ending in a pronounced black spot with a cream/yellow halo ate the base of the tail fin.

Size: Most range from 1-2 pounds. Catches of double that size aren't rare. Grows to a maximum of 28 inches.

Tackle and fishing: An outstanding sportfish that anglers travel long distances to target. They hit hard and fight extremely well. Most are fished for using fly and spin/baitcast outfits that also suit black bass fishing. A daylight feeding fish that is targeted using a variety of lures and big streamer flies. They will hit live baitfish.

Edibility: Very good. Most anglers practise catch release on this species.

Game status: Excellent.

CICHLID, RIO GRANDE

Scientific name: Herichthys cyanoguttatus. Also known as Rio Grande perch, pearl cichlid, Texas perch, Texas cichlid.

Range: Originally from the Rip Grande drainage in Texas near Brownsville.

The only cichlid species that is native to the lower United States. Due to introductions, this species is now widespread over the southern half of Texas, and is present in Florida, Louisiana and Arizona.

Habitat: Canals and brackish warm water mostly where there is in-stream brush and aquatic vegetation. They can tolerate high salinity levels. They are very sensitive to water temperatures below 49 degrees Fahrenheit.

Description: Cream and turquoise colored spots over a dark or light olive background. Some lightly shaded specimens feature five vertical darker bars along the rear of the body. The dorsal and anal fins are long and tapered. Male fish often develop a pronounced hump on the top of their head.

Size: Can grow to 10 inches in length. Most weigh around 6 ounces.

Tackle and fishing: Considered a good fighting fish for its size. They are easily caught with poles, fly or ultra light spin tackle. Typical panfish baits such as worms, crickets and minnows are productive as are small spinners, jigs and wet flies and poppers.

Edibility: Good.

Game status: Good

CISCO

Scientific name: Coregonus artedi. Also known as chub, lake herring, northern cisco, tullibee.

This is one of several closely related cisco species found throughout North America. C. artedi is the species most relevant to sportfishers.

Range: Widespread in Canada. Upper Mississippi basin, Great Lakes and eastward.

Habitat: A pelagic fish generally found in mid water zones of cold water lakes. In the north and west of its range it can be found in large rivers.

Description: A slender, cylindrical bodied fish with a bluish back and all over silver/pinkish iridescent sheen.

The walking catfish moves about on land with the aid of its stiff pectoral fins and a side-to-side body flexing motion.

Size: Generally around 1 pound but fish of twice that aren't uncommon. Can reach 6-7 pounds, especially in lakes.

Tackle and fishing: A popular ice fishing target. A good little fighting fish when taken on light outfits. Ultra light spin or fly tackle are the best for good sport, as is ice fishing. Tiny jigs, spinners and spoons are successful. Natural baits such as small minnows work well. Fly fishing with dry flies offers great fun when fish are feeding at the surface.

Edibility: Very good. Nice when smoked.

Game status: Very good. On light tackle.

CRAPPIE, BLACK

Scientific name: Also known as calico bass, crappie, speck, Oswego bass, grass bass, speckled bass, strawberry bass.

Range: Greatly expanded due to stocking. Now found throughout most of the United States.

Habitat: Prefers clear water in areas where there is abundant aquatic vegetation on sand and mud bottoms. Throughout ponds, rivers, lakes and sloughs where suitable habitat is located. Mostly found in deep water except when coming into shallower areas around 3-4 feet deep when spawning.

Description: A deep and laterally compressed body. A small head and arched back. A large mouth. The large dorsal and anal fins are almost symmetrical in shape. Coloring is dark gray/black mottling over a silver/gray base. The dorsal area can be greenish/olive. The dorsal, caudal and anal fins are clearly marked with black spots and patterning.

Very similar in appearance to the closely related white crappie (P. annularis)

Size: Can grow to 19 inches and 6 pounds. Most common from 8 ounces to 2 pounds in weight.

IGFA All-Tackle World Record 4 pound 8 ounces, Kerr Lake, VA, USA.

Tackle and fishing: An extremely important recreational sportfish. What it lacks in fight to some other panfish it makes up for in its eating qualities. Usually targeted with cane-poles or light spintackle. They are often fished for using small minnows as bait, but will hit other baits such as worms. Small spinners, spinnerbaits, feather jigs and crankbaits are all popular; they will also hit small streamers cast with flyrods. Trolling deepwater with diving plugs, spoons etc is effective.

Edibility: Excellent. Light colored, finely grained flesh without the 'fishy' taste that many people find distasteful.

Game status: Excellent.

CRAPPIE, WHITE

Scientific name: Also known as calico bass, crappie, speck, Oswego bass, grass bass, speckled bass, strawberry bass.

Range: The native range included the area west of the Appalachian Mountains north to southern Ontario and south to the Gulf of Mexico. Similar to the black crappie, due to stocking and becoming established, it now extends over most of the East and Midwest, and from the Gulf to southern Canada.

Habitat: Found in reservoirs, lakes and large rivers. They can survive in murky waters better than black crappie. Most commonly found in slower flowing areas in pools and backwaters. They frequent areas where there is plenty of cover such as logs, sunken tree tops, boat docks and brush piles.

Description: A deep-bodied fish with silver/green to dark green back. Silver coloration over the body with silver white belly area. Often has a pearlescent, or blue and purple sheen. Several darker vertical bars along the flanks. The best way to differentiate the white from the black crappie is that the white crappie has a maximum of 6 spines on the dorsal fin while the black crappie has more than six.

Size: Most fish are around ¾ to 1 pound, but fish of twice that size are common. IGFA All-Tackle World Record 5 pound 3 ounces, Enid Dam, MS, USA.

Tackle and fishing: Targeted for their eating qualities, rather than their fighting abilities that leave something to be desired. Depending on the season and the location of the fish, poles, spincasting a flyfishing are all productive methods when targeting white crappie. Tiny jigs, doll flies, small crankbaits, spoons, spinners and other lures will catch these fish, as will flies. Natural baits are probably the most productive however, and the use of live, medium sized minnows is the most successful.

Edibility: Excellent.

Game status: Average. Targeted for their excellent flesh.

DOLLY VARDEN

Scientific name: Salvenus malma.

Range: Coastal areas of Alaska from the southeast to the Gulf of Alaska and the Bearing Sea, into Beaufort Sea to the MacKenzie River in northern Canada. Also interior Alaska. Along the Pacific coast of North America from Washington State to the Arctic coast of Canada.

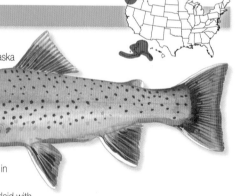

Habitat: Headwater streams to large deep lakes. Brackish estuaries and along shorelines. Some populations are totally landlocked and live entirely in streams or lakes.

Description: Sea fish are silvery all over with a greenish tinge overlaid with light orange spots. Freshwater fish can be confused with Arctic Char. Coloration is variable but mostly olive/gray/brown or pale silver/gray with white belly, overlaid with small orange/red spots.

Adult spawning fish (males are brighter) become brilliantly colored with red, black and white bellies with black gill covers and bright orange/red spots. Bright orange and black fins with clean white leading edges. Females are similar but not as brightly colored. Male spawning fish develop a strongly hooked kype.

Size: Varies depending on location. Small headwater fish may mature at 3-6 inches. Sea run and lake dwelling fish can grow to over 5 pounds.

IGFA All-Tackle World Record 20 pound 14 ounces, Wulik River, AK, USA.

Tackle and fishing: A solid but not flashy sporting fish. Spincasting, baitcasting and fly fishing tackle are all productive. They will hit spoons plugs, spinners and streamer flies. Natural baits include minnows and salmon eggs.

Edibility: Very good to excellent. Smoking enhances flavor of freshwater inhabiting fish.

Game status: Excellent.

DRUM, FRESHWATER

Scientific name: Aplodinotus grunniens. Also known as croaker, sheepshead, grunter, gray bass, drum fish, gou, gaspergou.

Range: A wide-ranging species. Hudson Bay to the Gulf of Mexico. Eastern Appalachians and west to Texas, Kansas and Oklahoma.

Habitat: Clean sand and gravel substrates in preferably clear water. They will tolerate turbid water however. Rivers and lakes. Widespread.

Description: The name grunter or croaker refers to the sound these fish make.

A deep bodied fish with a humped back, blunt snout and under slung lower jaw. The tail is pointed and the dorsal fin is long and divided into two sections. Similar in shape, but not coloration to the saltwater red drum. Color is silver on the sides and belly with a darker back.

Can be mistaken for carp or buffalo, however the drum has two dorsal fins whereas the others have only one.

Size: Most common to 10 pounds but can reach 50 plus pounds.

IGFA All-Tackle World Record 54 pound 8 ounces, Nickajack Lake, TN, USA.

Tackle and fishing: Many anglers consider these a 'trash' fish despite being tough, determined fighters and fair on the plate. They are a bottom feeder. Small specimens make good bait for other fish. They are often caught when anglers are targeting other, more popular species.

Caught on trotlines, spin and baitcasting tackle using baits such as worms and minnows, or artificial lures.

Edibility: Fair. White coarse flakes.

Game status: Very good. Underrated.

DRUM, RED

Scientific name: Scianops ocellatus. Also known as red bass, redfish, channel bass, drum, red, rat red.

Range: Cape cod, along the Atlantic Coast south, Gulf of Mexico. All Florida coasts. Keys.

Habitat: Across a wide range of coastal habitats including estuaries, river mouths, mud and sand flats, oyster beds, surf zones and outside beaches, bays and out to the continental shelf. Small fish mostly found over shallower waters and bigger fish in the surf zones and deeper gutters.

During cold weather they can be found in tidal creeks and rivers. They can exist in freshwater and are often located many miles upriver.

Description: Long fish with a sloping down head, blunt nose and under slung lower jaw. The Red Drum does not have barbels under the chin like the similar looking Black Drum. Usually a copper/red color on the back and upper sides. The lower sides and belly are whitish. Have a distinctive black spot near the base of the tail. One spot is usual but some fish have several spots at times.

Size: Often caught between 1 and 12 pound, but fish of twice that and greater aren't uncommon. Said to grow to 60 inches in length and attain a maximum weight of around 100 pound. IGFA All-Time World Record 94 pound 2 ounces, Avon, NC, USA.

Tackle and fishing: A solid, strong sportfish that gives a powerful and strong fight and usually performs long strong runs with the occasional jump.

Anglers fishing from beaches, piers or bridges use surf rods or light/medium saltwater outfits, although smaller fish can be targeted with lighter casting outfits including fly gear where appropriate. Redfish are fussy feeders and will eat many types of bait, live and dead, including small baitfish, crab, shrimp and cut baits. Surf anglers often use pieces of mullet and menhaden while shallow water fishers more often use crab, shrimp and small fish. Swimming lures and plugs, weedless spoons and plastic lures will take fish, as will poppers.

Edibility: Good. Small fish around 5-10 pound are best eating. Bigger fish aren't nice and should be released. Trim red flesh for best taste.

Game status: Very good.

EEL, AMERICAN

Scientific name: Anguilla rostrata. Also known as common eel, congo.

Range: All accessible east coast freshwater streams and lakes, coastal waters and estuaries of the entire Gulf. From Nova Scotia to Florida including the Great Lakes. One of the most widely distributed of all fish.

Habitat: Bottom dwellers that hide in snags, burrows and various protective shelters. There are few habitats they won't be found in. They hide in logs and under structure during the day and feed at night.

Description: A slender snake-like body that is covered with slime. A long dorsal fin that runs from the middle of the back to the meets up with the long ventral fin. Color varies from brown to greenish/yellow to olive green. The belly area is often white or light gray.

They rely heavily on their sense of smell to locate food.

Size: Normally around 24 inches but can grown to 3 plus feet in length.

IGFA All-Tackle World Record 9 pound 4 ounces, Cape May, NJ, USA.

Tackle and fishing: Usually taken by anglers fishing with bottom baits through the night. They will take a variety of different cut baits, worms and catfish baits depending on the area being fished. Their diet is extremely diverse and as such many baits will work.

American eels are important bait for anglers fishing along the east coast.

Edibility: Very good. Acquired taste.

Game status: Poor.

FALLFISH

Scientific name: Semotilus corporalis. Also known as chub, eastern chub, Mohawk chub, silver chub, white chub.

Range: Eastern Canada and north eastern United States.

Habitat: Streams, rivers and lake margins. Prefer rocky and gravel substrate.

Description: A slimy fish when held that makes a 'gurgling' sound when taken and held out of the water. A thick bodied minnow with pronounced silver scales below a brown/gray back. The scales often have blue/purple sheen. A large mouth with an overhanging top lip.

Size: Can grow to 10 inches.

Tackle and fishing: An important prey for larger fish. They make excellent bait and are mostly taken with nets or poles. They will hit flies, lures and baits.

Edibility: Poor.

Game status: Good. For their size. More important as bait.

FLIER

Scientific name: Centrarchus macropterus. Also known as flier perch, bream, round sunfish, millpond flier.

Range: Throughout south eastern United States. The deep south from Maryland to the Gulf.

Habitat: Prefer clear waters in sloughs, swamps, slow flowing creeks and streams. Highly acidic dark waters. Fish hang around stumps, sunken vegetation and under bridges etc.

They prefer water temperatures between 75 to 85 degrees Fahrenheit.

Description: They feature a deep, rounded body and large 'wing-like' dorsal fin. The anal fin is similar in shape and size to the dorsal fin. Superficially similar to the crappie in appearance. Coloration is olive green, brassy/olive to brownish/gold above, lighter green/yellow flanks, silvery white below. They have several rows of brown/black spots along the sides and over the large dorsal fin, and a dark vertical stripe below each eye.

Size: Generally caught around 5 inches but can reach 7-10 inches in length. Most weigh only 3 ounces.

Tackle and fishing: Another scrappy little fighter that is targeted more for its sweet eating than its fighting ability. Anglers targeting crappies probably catch most. Generally taken with poles and bait using small minnows, crickets, worms etc. They will hit flies (dries and wets) such as nymphs and micro spinners using spin or fly tackle.

Edibility: Excellent. Very sweet meat.

Game status: Good. Mostly taken to eat.

FLOUNDER, SOUTHERN

Scientific name: Paralichthys lethostigma. Also known as flattie, southern fluke, flounder, mud flounder.

Range: From Northern Carolina to Florida, and west to Texas. Rare in southern Florida.

Habitat: Lying or swimming along the bottom in shallow coastal areas. Often found in freshwater rivers that flow into its coastal range. Fish spawn at depths of 50-100 feet well offshore.

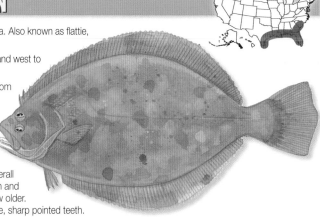

Description: A left-eye flounder, that is its eyes are always on the left hand side of the body. Laterally compressed body. Overall chocolate brownish with scattered larger tan and whitish spots that disappear as the fish grow older. Prominent eyes and a large mouth with large, sharp pointed teeth.

Size: Average between 2-3 pounds, bit can grow to twice that or more. Females typically grow to about 28 inches in length. Male fish rarely exceed 12 inches.

IGFA All-Tackle World Record 20 pound 9 ounces, Nassau Sound, FL, USA.

Tackle and fishing: A solid fighting fish that hits hard. Taken with light spin, baitcasting tackle using artificial lures and natural baits. Plastic worm jigs and spoons are effective. Live or dead baits are very effective, especially live minnows and shrimp.

Edibility: Excellent.

Game status: Excellent.

GAR, ALLIGATOR

Scientific name: Lepisosteus spatula. Also known as great gar, gator gar, manjuari, gaspar, catan.

Range: Northern Gulf Coast from the Econfina River in Florida south to Veracruz, Mexico.

Habitat: Large rivers and reservoirs and occasionally into coastal bays.

Description: Easily distinguished from other species by their long, cylindrical bodies, long, wide snouts and double rows of teeth on both sides of the top jaw.

Diamond shaped scales and rounded tail. Color is usually brown or olive above and lighter below and the dorsal and anal fins are set well back on the body and almost exactly opposite each other.

Size: A fast growing but slow spawning fish. They have been known to reach 327 pounds in weight and over 10 feet in length. Most caught are far less and probably average 20-50 pounds.

IGFA All-Tackle World Record 279 pound, Rio Grande, Texas, USA.

Tackle and fishing: A solid fighter if simply because of its size. Even so, it's no slouch and gives a good account of itself. Usually taken on heavy fresh or saltwater tackle using live fish baits below floats. Have been known to hit lures from time to time. Often targeted by Bow anglers.

Edibility: Rarely eaten.

Game status: Excellent. A tough brawler.

GAR, FLORIDA

Scientific name: Lepisosteus platyrhincus. Also known as garfish.

Range: Ochlockonee River drainage, and waters east of, and including the Florida peninsula.

Habitat: Medium to large lowland streams, canals and lakes with muddy and sand bottoms and aquatic vegetation. Often found near the surface where anglers can spot them.

Description: Olive/brown on the back and sides with a white/yellow lower body and belly. Irregular round black spots over the body, head, tail and fins. An elongated, broad snout with nostrils at the tip, and with a single row of sharp teeth in both jaws. The body is covered in extremely hard, diamond shaped plates. Best distinguished from the spotted gar by the snout lengths.

Size: A mid sized gar that weighs between 2-10 pounds.

IGFA All-Tackle World Record 10 pounds, The Everglades, FL, USA.

Tackle and fishing: A good fighting fish that can be taken using fly, spin, baitcast tackle or poles. Most are caught using live or dead minnows and other baits. They will hit flies and artificial offerings as well on occasions.

Edibility: Rarely eaten. Roe is toxic to humans and animals.

Game status: Very good. Especially bigger specimens.

GAR, LONGNOSE

Scientific name: Lepisosteus osseus. Also known as needlenose, garfish, needlenosed gar, bonypike.

Range: Frequently found in waters in the eastern half of the United States. St.Lawrence River in Quebec and south to central Florida. As far west as Kansas and Texas and southern New Mexico.

Habitat: Mostly freshwater but also into brackish estuaries and inlets. They frequent areas around drowned trees and vegetation and rocky outcrops in slow moving streams, rivers, lakes, bayous and estuaries. Often located floating near the surface.

Description: A long cylindrical body and long snout that is more than twice the length of the rest of its head. They have only

GAR, LONGNOSE CONTINUED...

one row of sharp teeth in the upper jaw, which helps it to be distinguished from the alligator gar, which has two rows on either side.

Coloration is variable depending on water clarity, deep olive green/brown above fading to pale yellow/white below in clear water and more subdued in murky waters. Some irregular dark spotting over the body, plus also on the dorsal, anal and caudal fins.

Size: Slow growing and long lived fish. They can reach 6'8" in length and 35 pounds in weight. Most fish caught would be around 1/3 of that weight.

IGFA All-Tackle World Record 50 pound 5 ounces, Trinity River, TX, USA.

Tackle and fishing: An exciting if short lived fight. Their sharp teeth and head shaking antics when hooked require the use of wire leaders to avoid being cut off. Anglers should also handle caught fish with care to avoid be cut by the sharp teeth. They are often bowfished. Spin, baitcast and fly tackle are all suitable. Most are taken on natural live or dead, or cut fish baits. They will hit lures and flies.

Edibility: Good.

Game status: Good. Often seen as a nuisance fish by anglers chasing other sportfish.

GAR, SHORTNOSE

Scientific name: Lepisosteus platostomus. Also known as garfish, Billy gar, stubnose gar, short-billed gar.

Range: Mississippi River drainage from the Gulf Coast as far north as Montana in the west and the Ohio River in the east.

Habitat: Large rivers, oxbows, lakes and quite backwaters. Very tolerant of highly turbid waters.

Description: They lack the double row of teeth in the upper jaw of the alligator gar, the spots of the longnose gar, or the long snout of the longnose gar.

Color varies from olive-green to brown dorsally with yellow sides and white belly.

Size: Can grow to about 5 pounds and 35 inches. Most are around 2 pounds and 24 inches.

IGFA All-Tackle World Record 5 pound 12 ounces, Rend Lake, IL, USA.

Tackle and fishing: Not much of a fight. Bowfishing is popular on this species. Tackled with poles, spin, bait and fly casting tackle using natural baits such as cut fish, minnows, worms or small spinners and wet flies.

Edibility: Fair. Too small for a decent feed.

Game status: Fair.

GAR, SPOTTED

Scientific name: Lepisosteus oculatus.

Range: Wide ranging from the Great Lakes down to the Gulf of Mexico. Mississippi River drainage. Central Texas into western Florida.

Habitat: Occasionally into brackish waters along the Gulf Coast, but mostly in clear, calm and well vegetated streams, lakes and swamps. Often floating near the surface on warm days.

Description: A long cylindrical body. Coloration is brown/tan to olive above with silver/white/cream flanks and belly. The head, back and fins have olive/brown to black spots. They can be distinguished from other gars by the roundish dark spots on the head, pectoral and pelvic fins.

Size: Can attain 8 pounds and grow to 3 feet in length. Most are around 2-3 pounds in weight.

IGFA All-Tackle World Record 9 pound 12 ounces, Lake Mexia, TX, USA.

Tackle and fishing: Not recognised for its fight. They can be taken using poles, spin, baitcast and fly tackle. Most commonly caught using baits such as worms, minnows and cut baits. They will hit lures and flies at times.

Edibility: Poor. Roe is poisonous to humans.

Game status: Average.

GOBY, ROUND

Scientific name: Neogobius melanostomus.

Range: A non-native species introduced by accident into the United States. A Eurasian fish species. Found in the Great Lakes and expanding into tributaries.

Habitat: Found in both fresh and marine environments. Often around rock and sand bar areas.

Description: A small, soft bodied fish with a very distinctive black spot on the rear end of the first dorsal fin. They have a large head and protruding eyes at the top of the head. Coloration is a mottled green, brown, black and gray overall with a whitish belly.

Size: Grow to around 4-10 inches.

IGFA All-Tackle World Record 10 pounds, The Everglades, FL, USA.

Tackle and fishing: Will hit lures, flies and baits but they aren't targeted by anglers and they put up little resistance. If caught should be killed and not released.

Edibility: Poor.

Game status: N/A.

GOLDEYE

Scientific name: Hiodon alosoides. Also known as western goldeye, yellow herring, toothed herring, Winnipeg goldeye, shad moponeye.

Range: Arctic and across Canada. From Louisiana to Minnesota in the Mississippi River system. Missouri and Ohio Rivers.

Habitat: Prefers turbid, warm, silty, slow flowing rivers and shallow lakes. They also inhabit marshes, ponds and muddy lakes shallows. Mostly a surface feeding fish.

Description: A small, blunt headed fish with a large mouth that extends to the rear of the eye and is full of teeth. Conspicuous is the yellow/gold iris of the eye that helps it see in low light and turbid water. A deep body, that varies in color from dark blue to blue/green above with silver sides and white belly. Scales are edged in brown which shows as a tan appearance overall.

Size: Usually less than 1 pound.

Tackle and fishing: There small size limits their fishing appeal although they are popular with flyfishers. They give a good account of themselves on ultra light spin and fly tackle and are also taken with poles. They take dry flies and natural insect baits.

Edibility: Fair.

Game status: Good. On ultra light tackle.

GOLDFISH

Scientific name: Carassius auratus.

Range: A native fish of eastern Asia, including China. Widespread across the United States due to releasing of unwanted aquarium fish, or those used for bait into waterways.

Habitat: Mostly ponds, slow flowing, warm waterways where there is aquatic vegetation and mud substrate.

Description: These fish have been domesticated and bred for thousands of years and many color variations exist. Color can be gray, brassy or silver in wild fish, but there are also many that are red, orange or yellow/gold. A deep, fat bodied fish with a small mouth and large flowing dorsal and tail fins.

Size: Most are only a few ounces but they can grow to around 15 inches and 5 pounds.

IGFA All-Tackle World Record 6 pound 10 ounces, Lake Hodges, CA, USA.

Tackle and fishing: Not a sporting fish, fun for kids to catch using poles and small hooks baited with worms, dough, cheese, corn etc.

Edibility: N/A.

Game status: N/A. Not big enough.

GRAYLING, ARCTIC

Scientific name: Thymallus arcticus. Also known as grayling, Montana grayling, American grayling.

Range: Native to the Arctic Ocean, northern Pacific Ocean in North America and Hudson Bay. There are two distinct populations in Michigan (now extinct) and Montana. The only remaining natural remaining population in the continental United States is in the Big Hole River, Montana. Introduced (or re-introduced) elsewhere.

Habitat: In clear streams, rivers and lakes. Fish often school.

Description: Easily identified fish due to its sail-like dorsal fin. A slender body, short head and large eyes. A vividly colored fish, especially at spawning times. Color can vary due to location. Mostly overall dull metallic gray or brassy color, or purplish blue with scattered black spots on sides. The dorsal fin is purple or blue/black and has rows of orange or emerald green spots edged with orange on the male fish.

Size: Most fish are less than 16 inches and less than 2 pounds.

IGFA All-Tackle World Record 5 pound 15 ounces, Katseyedie River, N.W.T.

Tackle and fishing: A great little sportfish on ultra light spin and fly tackle. Most are targeted by fly anglers using light outfits and small dry flies. Lure anglers take fish on very small spinners and spoons.

Edibility: Excellent. Most fish are returned to the water.

Game status: Excellent. A prime fly fishing target.

GUAPOTE, JAGUAR

Scientific name: Cichlasoma managuense.

Range: A native fish of South America.

Mostly throughout coastal canal systems of southeast Florida. Ranging as far north as West Palm Beach. Cold temperatures restrict northern expansion.

Habitat: Tolerates poor quality water, usually found in canals.

Description: Body coloration is olive/brown/ purple above shading to lighter below. A purplish sheen with numerous purple to black spots and blotches over body and fins and a row of black 'squares' along the flank. A large mouth with distinct teeth. The body patterning makes this species very distinct.

Size: Usually less than 1 pound but have been caught to 16 inches and 2.8 pounds.

Tackle and fishing: An aggressive and strong fish that will take live small fish, worms, small spinners and other artificial baits, streamer flies, poppers and surface plugs.

Poles, light spin and fly tackle are all used.

Edibility: Excellent.

Game status: Very good.

HARDHEAD

Scientific name: Mylopharodon conocephalus. Also known as California hardhead.

Range: Pit River system and the drainages of the Russian, Joaquin and Sacramento Rivers.

Habitat: Low to mid elevation, small to large streams. Possibly lakes as well.

Description: Large, slender minnow with a slightly deeper body than the Sacramento pikeminnow. Color is dusky bronze/brown on the back with silver sides.

Size: Mostly around 12 inches but can reach 24 inches.

Tackle and fishing: Bigger fish are fun to catch. Mostly takes baits such as worms, shellfish and cut baits.

Edibility: Good.

Game status: Good. When larger in size.

HERRING, BLUEBACK

Scientific name: Alosa aestivalis. Also known as blueback shad, river herring, summer herring, blue herring.

Range: coast from Nova Scotia to St.Johns River, Florida.

Habitat: Open seas, entering estuaries and ascending coastal rivers during spawning. Inland rivers and lakes. They prefer hard bottoms of clay or gravel in lakes. They are a problem fish in lakes where they predate on the eggs and fry of popular sportfish such as largemouth bass and walleye.

Description: Silver color overall with deep bluish/green back. Small dark spot immediately behind the gill plate. The body has a series of scutes along the belly. Distinguished by the black or dusky colored internal belly cavity area.

Hard to distinguish from the Alewife (Alosa pseudoharengus). The alewife has larger eyes and deeper body.

Size: Can grow to 16 inches in length. Most are less than 12 inches.

Tackle and fishing: Good fun on very light tackle. Usually caught by kids fishing with small hooks baited with shrimp or pieces of squid or fish.

Sometimes targeted for use as bait. The use of these fish as live bait in some lakes is illegal.

Edibility: Good.

Game status: Good. Fun on light tackle.

HERRING, SKIPJACK

Scientific name: Alosa chrysochloris. Also known as golden shad.

Range: Gulf of Mexico drainages. Mississippi River and its major tributaries to South Dakota.

Habitat: A migratory schooling fish that enters brackish and freshwater. They prefer large rivers with fast flowing water (clear to moderately turbid) and lakes. Throughout mid water and the surface.

Description: Laterally compressed, narrow-bodied fish with a blue/green back and bright silver flanks and belly. Not as deep bodied as the Alabama shad. Along the belly they have a row of scales folded over on the edge that create points. Black pigment on the point of the lower jaw, which protrudes considerably past the upper jaw. They have a large mouth.

Young skipjack and Alabama shad are very similar in appearance.

Size: Usually 12-16 inches in length, but can reach 21 inches and 3.5 pounds in weight.

Tackle and fishing: An acrobatic fish that puts up a good fight on ultra light spin and fly tackle. They will hit live minnows, lures and streamer flies.

Edibility: Good. Very bony though.

Game status: Very good. On light tackle.

INCONNU (SHEERFISH)

Scientific name: Stenodus leucichthys. Also known as sheerfish, coney, cony, conny, Eskimo tarpon.

Range: Northwestern North America and the Arctic drainages of Alaska.

Habitat: A freshwater migratory fish (do not run to sea). Thought to remain in their spawning rivers for two years before descending to larger lakes.

Description: A large fish with a long, shallow head. Lower jaw projects past the upper jaw that resembles that of a tarpon. Overall coloring is silver with a pale green or brown back and white belly. The dorsal fin is set back along the body and the tail is distinctly forked.

Size: A large fish where 10-20 pounders are reasonably common. Can grow to over 50 pounds in weight.

IGFA All-Tackle World Record 53 pounds, Pah River, AK, USA.

Tackle and fishing: Most fish are caught in gill nets during downstream migrations and rarely targeted by recreational anglers. They are extremely hard fighting fish that run long and deep.

Anglers catch them on spin tackle using various spoons and spinners. Fly fishers using streamers also catch them.

Edibility: Good. Very oily flesh, better smoked.

Game status: Very good. Underrated recreational fish.

KILLIFISH, BANDED

Scientific name: Fundulus diaphanous. Also known as killie.

Range: Coastal drainages from Newfoundland to South Carolina, and west to Minnesota. The Great Lakes. And Mississippi drainages.

The only killifish found in the north eastern United States.

Habitat: Primarily a freshwater fish that is sometimes found in brackish environments. Lakes, ponds and slow flowing streams, usually close to aquatic vegetation.

Description: A slender, elongated fish with a flattened head and upward sloping mouth.

Olive above and sides and white along the belly. Throat and fins are yellowish. Several vertical, alternating black and silver/white stripes running along the body.

Size: Between 2-5 inches.

Tackle and fishing: Can be taken with small baits and hooks but not considered a recreational fish species. Most are targeted for use as bait for larger fish using nets.

Edibility: N/A.

Game status: N/A. Good for use as bait.

LADYFISH

Scientific name: Elopssaurus. Also known as ten pounder, chiro, big-eyed herring, silverfish.

Range: Cape Cod to Gulf of Mexico. All Florida coasts, Bahamas and Caribbean. Bermuda.

Habitat: Found in brackish waters throughout lagoons, estuaries, bays, canals and mangroves. Occasionally some distance offshore, and also occasionally in freshwater.

LADYFISH CONTINUED...

Description: A long, slender fish with a very large and deeply forked tail fin. Silver/blue/green above with bright silver sides and belly. Dorsal and tail fins shaded yellow. Body is covered with numerous small scales. Head is small and pointed.

Size: Usually caught between 1-2 pound with bigger fish uncommon. Can grow to 3 feet with a maximum weight of 15 pounds.

Tackle and fishing: Wild leaps and acrobatics are typical when these fish are hooked. When they finally settle down and swim, they give fast, strong runs for their small size on light tackle. They are great, light line, shallow water sportfish.

Can be caught using baitcasting, spinning and flyfishing outfits. They willingly hit small flashy lures, flashy streamer flies, jigs and poppers. Often caught on small strip baits, live shrimp and small baitfish when targeting other species.

Edibility: N/A. Rarely eaten and very bony.

Game status: Very good. Great fun on ultra light tackle.

LAMPREY, SEA

Scientific name: Petromyzon marinus. Also known as lamprey eel.

Range: Considered a pest species in many areas where it predates on trout and other game fish. Atlantic rivers and lakes throughout North America.

Habitat: An invasive species that will move about in search of host fish.

Description: Eel-like in appearance. A sucking disc at the head that allows the lamprey to attach itself to the host fish. Mottled black/brown/olive on the back and sides, lighter on the belly.

Size: Generally under 2 feet.

Tackle and fishing: Not targeted by anglers.

Edibility: Poor.

Game status: N/A.

MINNOW, SHEEPSHEAD

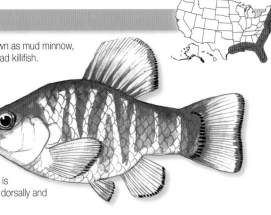

Scientific name: Cyprinodon variegates. Also known as mud minnow, variegated minnow, chubby, sheepshead pupfish, broad killifish.

Range: Atlantic Coast and the Gulf of Mexico.

Habitat: Fresh and saltwater habitats. Prefer quite, shallow waters in saltwater bays and estuaries, creeks, canals and ditches with sand and silt bottoms.

Often kept as an aquarium fish.

Description: A deep-bodied fish with a small flattened head and arched back. A small mouth. Large pectoral fins and small pelvic fins. Body is covered in large scales. Coloration is olive green/gray dorsally and yellowish/silver below.

Size: Generally 2 inches but can reach 10 inches in length.

Tackle and fishing: No recreational use apart from being very good bait for larger fish. Most are taken with nets or in minnow traps.

Edibility: N/A.

Game status: N/A. Good bait.

MOONEYE

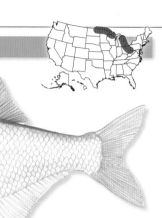

Scientific name: Hiodon tergisus. Also known big eyed shad, toothed herring, white shad.

Range: South-central Canada to the Great Lakes (except Lake Superior). St.Lawrence River and Lake Champlain drainage basin. Ohio valley into Mississippi.

Populations of mooneye are dwindling in numbers and locations.

Habitat: Prefer clear waters in large streams, rivers and lakes. Mostly surface feeders.

Description: A flattened, deep bodied fish that is silver in color with blue/green back. Similar in appearance to the goldeye, but with a smaller mouth and jaw that doesn't reach back past the eyes. Large eyes, small head and a small, fleshy flap just above the pelvic fins. It has teeth on the tongue and also on the inside roof of its mouth.

Size: Usually between 11-15 inches in length and 1-2 pounds in weight.

Tackle and fishing: A solid little fighter when hooked on ultra light spin and fly tackle. They will hit small spoons, jigs and dry and wet flies, plus natural insect baits.

Edibility: Poor. Flesh is soft and bony and not very tasty.

Game status: Good. On ultra light tackle.

MULLET, STRIPED

Scientific name: Mugil cephalus. Also known as mullet, jumping mullet, black mullet, black back mullet, common mullet.

Range: Common worldwide. In the western Atlantic Ocean they range from Nova Scotia south to Brazil, including the Gulf. Southern California and the Colorado River. Often found long distances up streams and in some landlocked systems.

Habitat: A variety of habitats including the ocean, estuaries, salt marshes, lagoons and freshwater rivers and creeks with sand, mud or vegetated bottoms. Highly salty to freshwater environs. From the surface to the bottom, throughout the water column.

Description: Silver body with dark bluish-gray/green back and dark horizontal stripes along the sides. Belly is white. The mouth is small, the nose blunt and the tail deeply forked.

Size: Usually ½ to 2 pounds. Can reach double that weight.

Tackle and fishing: They are a common prey item for many predatory fish and are therefore a popular baitfish. Fun fish to catch in their own right, especially by children. Spin tackle, poles and fly tackle are all used. Small pieces of bacon dough, shrimp and corn, earthworms and oatmeal are all popular baits, especially when fished under a float in conjunction with berley. Small wet or dry flies are often successful.

Edibility: Excellent. Fish caught in freshwater not so much as they often have a muddy taste.

Game status: Poor. Mostly targeted as bait for larger fish.

MUMMICHOG

Scientific name: Fundulus heteroclitus. Also known as killifish, mud minnow, marsh minnow, mummy, gudgeon, mud dabbler, saltwater minnow, brackish water chub.

Range: Atlantic coast drainages from Labrador to Florida.

Habitat: Brackish coastal waters including estuaries, marshes and into freshwater. Near the bottom over muddy substrates.

Description: Elongate but fat body with a blunt head an upturned mouth. The lower jaw projects past the upper jaw. Coloring is generally olive/brown to olive/green but variable. They often have wavy, thin vertical bars on the flanks that are a silvery color. Breeding males are far more colourful with dark green backs and steel blue flanks with silvery bars and a yellow/orange belly area.

Size: Generally 2-3 inches but can reach 6 inches in length.

Tackle and fishing: Not a recreational fish. Usually caught with nets for use as bait. Will take small cut baits fished with poles.

Edibility: N/A.

Game status: N/A. Good as bait.

MUSKELLUNGE

Scientific name: Esox masquinongy. Also known as muskie, musky, green pike, muskellunge, muscallonge, maskinonge, milliganong, barred muskellunge.

Range: Northern Michigan, northern Minnesota, Great Lakes and into Canada. From the St. Lawrence River drainage and through the upper Mississippi valley and as far south as Chattanooga.

Habitat: Prefer clear waters in lakes and large rivers where they hold up along the edge of weed beds, rocky outcrops and other structure. They will often go deep to escape the heat and at these times they tend to hunt around structure and edge drop offs.

In rivers they tend to hunt around and hold around submerged structure such as logs in slower areas and eddies. They are ambush predators. They sometimes school.

Description: They closely resemble American pickerel and northern pike in appearance and hunting behaviour. They have an elongated body, flat head and long underslung jaw filled with sharp teeth. Their dorsal anal and pelvic fins are set well back along the body as per other pike.

Color varies somewhat depending on the environment, but mostly they are silver, green or brown above with yellowish sides and dark vertical stripes along the flanks.

Muskellunge have seven or more sensory pores (along each side) along the underside of the mandible. Northern pike never have more than five on each side.

Size: The largest fish in the pike family. Typically they range between 28-48 inches in length and between 5-35 pound. They can reach 6 feet and almost 70 pound.

IGFA All-Tackle World Record 67 pound 8 ounces, Hayward, WI, USA.

Tackle and fishing: One of the toughest, they are an apex predator. The fight is usually, strong, violent and acrobatic with head shaking leaps. Quality, strong baitcast, spin or fly gear is needed to subdue these great sportfish. Muskie's don't come easily, and often require numerous casts to elicit a strike.

Live baitfish (around 8-10 inches in length) are top baits, either drifted or trolled. Large, noisy surface plugs are popular, as are jerkbaits and bucktail spinners. Very large lures around 12-20 inches are often used.

Flyfishing with large streamer flies can be successful if the angler is prepared to put in hundreds of casts.

Edibility: Very good. Most fish are released to grow bigger and preserve the population.

Game status: Exceptional. One of the best.

MUSKELLUNGE, TIGER

Scientific name: Esox lucius x Esox masquinongy. Also known as hybrid musky, tiger musky, tiger muskie.

Range: Similar to Muskellunge. Tiger muskellunge are often stocked into waters where muskellunge can't breed naturally. There is some natural hybridization that takes place where northern pike and muskellunge populations overlap.

Habitat: Similar habitat to muskellunge.
Often in shallow weedy bays, around structure such as sunken logs and docks, or deeper along steeper drop-offs and shelves.

Description: A sterile cross between northern pike and muskellunge. As with other members of the pike family, they all have a similar appearance. Tiger muskies have dark spots(in juveniles) or vertical darker bars or stripes over a light background in adults. The tips of the tail are rounded in tigers, in pure muskies they are pointed.

Size: Generally slightly smaller than muskellunge. Mature fish are 34-48 inches in length and can grow to more than 30 pounds in weight. IGFA All-Tackle World Record 51 pound 3 ounces, Lac Vieux-Desert, WI-MI, USA.

Tackle and fishing: The title of 'fish of 1000 casts' has been bestowed on this fish due to the time and effort required to get a response from these rugged, flashy fighters. They are top predators that feed on large fish when available and as such anglers often use very large lures to mimic that prey.

Strong gear such as baitcast, spin and even fly tackle is necessary to cast big rigs and subdue these brawlers.

Popular lures include glide baits, jerk baits, bucktail spinners, spinnerbaits, plugs and spoons. Live baits such as suckers and other large live baitfish are the best.

Edibility: Very good. Must be released quickly and unharmed in many areas. Most anglers return fish whether it's the law or not.

Game status: Exceptional. A true sportfish.

NEEDLEFISH, ATLANTIC

Scientific name: Strongylura marina. Also known as agujon, billfish, bluebone, garfish, silver gar, northern needlefish, saltwater gar.

Range: Nova Scotia to southern Brazil. Coast of Gulf of Mexico and Caribbean.

Habitat: Ocean waters, estuaries and coastal streams including well upstream in freshwater. Common around marinas and areas with minimal current flows.

A surface swimming fish often seen around docks, marshes, beaches and grass beds.

Description: Extremely long jaws with numerous small sharp (needle like) teeth. Long slender body is translucent with a light yellow/greenish back with silver sides and bluish/silver stripe along each side. One dorsal fin located far along the back near the tail. The fins are yellowish along the edges.

Size: Can grow to around 36 inches but most are caught below 12 inches in length.

Tackle and fishing: Can be fun for kids on ultra light lines and small cut baits. Rarely large enough for any real fight. Usually caught with nets for use as bait.

Edibility: Poor.

Game status: Poor. Used for bait.

OSCAR

Scientific name: Astrontus ocellatus. Also known as velvet cichlid, tiger oscar, marble cichlid.

Range: A native of South America. A popular aquarium fish that is now widespread in some areas of the United States, including Hawaii and southward from lake Okeechobee Florida. Its intolerance for cooler waters limits its northward push in the United States.

Habitat: Mostly sluggish and slow-moving, well vegetated waters, often sheltering around submerged branches.

Description: Wild populations are usually dark brown with yellow bars and mottling. They have a black spot haloed with red/yellow on the base of the tail fin and often two or three along the base of the dorsal fin. They can rapidly change their coloring during territorial disputes.

OSCAR CONTINUED...

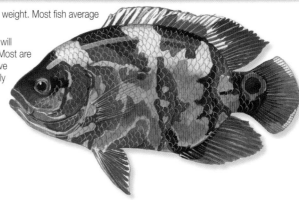

Size: Can grow to 18 inches and 3.5 pounds in weight. Most fish average between 8 ounces and 1 pound.

Tackle and fishing: A strong little fighter that will aggressively hit natural baits and artificial lures. Most are taken using poles, light spin or fly tackle. Small live minnows and worms are popular natural baits. Fly anglers use streamer flies and popping bugs to good effect and lure anglers take fish on small plugs, spinners and soft plastics.

Edibility: Very good.

Game status: Good.

PADDLEFISH

Scientific name: Polyodon spathula. Also known as shovelnose, spoonbill, Mississippi paddlefish, spoonbilled cat.

Range: Native to the Mississippi River basin. Populations have declined dramatically due to overfishing, pollution and habitat destruction. A highly mobile fish.

Habitat: Large, free-flowing rivers and impoundments. Most frequently in deep, slow current areas in side channels, bayous, oxbows and dam tailwaters.

Description: Unmistakable fishes whose fossil records can be traced back some 300 million years. A smooth skinned fish that feeds primarily on zooplankton. They have a large mouth and paddle shaped nose and deeply forked tail fin. Coloration is a dull bluish/gray, often with some mottling and a whitish belly area.

Size: Most fish run between 20-50 pounds. The largest ever taken was 85 inches long and weighed 198 pounds.

Tackle and fishing: Paddlefish are filter feeders and as such don't take baits or lures. A popular angling fish where their numbers and regulations permit their capture. They are caught by snagging with weighted treble hooks using heavy spin or baitcasting outfits. Because they are large, foul hooked and often hooked in flowing water, they take some effort to land.

Many paddlefish are often illegally targeted for their caviar.

Edibility: Excellent.

Game status: Excellent.

PEAMOUTH

Scientific name: Mylocheilus caurinus. Also known as peamouth chub, northwest dace.

Range: Rivers and lakes of northwestern North America.

Habitat: Lakes and slow flowing rivers. Can tolerate diluted seawater and can be found in estuaries. A schooling fish.

Description: A slender fish with a dark brown or silver/gray back and silvery flanks and white belly. Two dark, dusky stripes along the flanks and reddish corners to the mouth. Breeding fish have a red midside stripe as well. Fins are yellow/orange. They have a small barbell on each side of the mouth.

Size: Mostly between 4-7 inches but can reach 14 inches in length.

Tackle and fishing: Not large enough for a fight but will readily eat small baits such as worms, bread, dough, roe and aquatic insects. Can be eaten, but most are caught for use as bait for larger fish.

Easily caught from piers, riverbanks and lakeshores around structure such as rock piles etc. Will take small wet flies.

Edibility: N/A. Taken for use as bait.

Game status: N/A.

PERCH, SACRAMENTO

Scientific name: Archoplites interruptus.

Range: Widely introduced throughout the western United States. Native to the Sacramento-San Joaquin, Pajaro and Salinas River areas of California. Now rare in their native waters.

Habitat: Preferred habitat is sluggish, well-vegetated sloughs, rivers and lakes. Often along the bottom of inshore lake areas.

Description: A deep bodied fish with a large mouth and upper jaw extending to the middle of the eye. Coloration is brown on the sides and back with metallic green/purple sheen. There are 6-7 vertical bars along the flanks and a black spot on the opercula and a darker line running back from the eye. Belly is white.

Size: Can reach 24 inches in length and 7.9 pounds in weight.

Tackle and fishing: A strong fighting fish that is mostly caught using spin and baitcasting outfits and spinner lures. They will eat small baitfish, crickets and worms.

Edibility: Very good.

Game status: Very good.

PERCH, SILVER

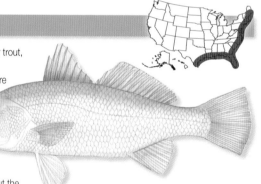

Scientific name: Bairdiella chrysoura. Also known as silver trout, yellowtail.

Range: Western Atlantic. New York to southern Florida. Inshore waters of Florida. Eastern and northern Gulf of Mexico to northern Mexico. During cold weather periods it often roams some distance up coastal rivers and streams into freshwater.

Habitat: Schools in big numbers and found in numbers along coastal streams and rivers. Usually over sandy and mud bottoms and seagrass beds.

Description: Often confused with Silver Seatrout but without the canine teeth. Gray/black/brown back with silver or yellowish sides and belly. Fins have yellowish or gray tinged. No barbels on chin.

Size: Normally around 6 inches and rarely bigger.

Tackle and fishing: Not large enough to offer any real sport. Makes up for that with its eating qualities. Will hit very small jigs and lures and fish bit pieces, shrimp or squid on small hooks using light spinning tackle.

Edibility: Excellent.

Game status: Too small to rate.

PERCH, WHITE

Scientific name: Morone Americana. Also known as sea perch, narrow-mouthed bass.

Range: From Nova Scotia to South Carolina. Most abundant from the Hudson River to Chesapeake Bay.

Habitat: Migrate to tidal fresh and slightly brackish water to spawn each spring. Widespread throughout their inshore range in estuaries, bays and streams, but less so along outer coastal areas.

Description: Closely related to striped bass but only vaguely similar in appearance. Young fish are marked with irregular dusky longitudinal stripes but these fade by adulthood. Dorsal area is darkish with the body showing an overall greenish/white coloring. The fish has two distinct dorsal fins and the anal fin possesses three prominent strong spines. The fish has a slightly projecting lower jaw.

Size: Most commonly found around 7-10 inches and weighing less than one pound. Maximum weight around 5 pound.

IGFA All-Tackle World Record 3 pound 1 ounce, Forest Hill Park, NJ, USA.

Tackle and fishing: Offers good fun on ultra light spin and fly tackle. An important recreational species that are often caught on a wide range of tackle. Often caught on minnows or insects, with the best catches occurring during the spawning season from September through November. Can be caught from the shore or from boats as they range throughout a wide area and variety of habitats.

Edibility: Excellent.

Game status: Good. Best when caught on ultra light tackle.

PICKEREL, CHAIN

Scientific name: Esox niger. Also known as pike, jack, lake pickerel, eastern pickerel, chainsides, jackfish.

Range: New Brunswick and south to Florida. Alabama and Mississippi basin and north to Southern Missouri, Kentucky and Illinois. Native to the Piedmont and coastal Plain of North Carolina. Other Atlantic and Gulf Coast drainages from New England to western Louisiana.

Habitat: Throughout aquatic vegetated lakes, ponds, swamps and backwaters of large and small rivers. Around weed beds, lily pads and snag areas. Prefers shallow water areas.

Description: A solitary fish. It is a member of the pike family. Deep olive green back with lighter yellowish sides overlaid with darker 'chain-like' markings. Belly is creamy yellow/white. Black vertical mark under each eye. Scales on cheeks and gill covers.

Size: Usually between 1-3 pounds but can grow to around 9 pounds. Considered big at 27 inches and 4 pounds.

IGFA All-Tackle World Record 9 pound 6 ounces, Homerville, GA, USA.

Tackle and fishing: A spirited fighting fish that hits lures, flies and baits ferociously. Best when taken on light tackle. They are often taken by bass anglers casting plugs, but also hit spinnerbaits, spoons, jigs, crankbaits, flies, bucktails and surface plugs. They will eat live minnow baits and pork rind baits.

Edibility: Excellent. White flesh but bony.

Game status: Excellent. On light tackle.

PICKEREL, REDFIN

Scientific name: Esox americanus americanus. Also known as grass pickerel, little pickerel, barred pickerel, redfinned pike, mud pickerel.

Range: Same territory as the chain pickerel but wider distribution in the Midwest, from the Great Lakes to East Texas, Kansas, Nebraska and Oklahoma.

Habitat: In clear streams with slow to moderate currents, undercut banks and abundant aquatic vegetation. In small ponds, swamps and lakes around the vegetated edges of lakes. Adults are solitary fish.

Description: Elongated body with a short and broad duckbill like snout. A dark backward (can be vertical) slanting bar beneath the eye.

Colors can vary. The back is dark green or brown, fading down the flanks with a cream or white belly area. Forward slanting green bars over the lighter colored sides. The cheeks and gill covers are fully scaled. The fins are reddish/orange.

Size: Can exceed 1 pound at times, but mostly restricted from 4-15 inches in lengt hand rarely exceed 12 inches.

IGFA All-Tackle World Record 2 pound 4 ounces, Gall Berry Swamp, NC, USA.

Tackle and fishing: An aggressive predator, but too small to offer any real sport. They are taken with poles and light spinning tackle using minnows, fish strips and weedless lures. They hit lures that are being retrieved fairly rapidly past weedbeds and tree structure.

Edibility: Good. But Bony.

Game status: Fair. Mostly too small.

PIKE, NORTHERN

Scientific name: Esox lucius. Also known as jack, jackfish, pickerel, northern, pike.

Range: Most of Canada, and most parts of the U.S.A. including Alaska.

Habitat: Similar habitat to the muskellunge. Sluggish streams and shallow weedy habitat in lakes. They are ambush predators that lie completely still for long periods around structure while waiting for prey to swim past.

Description: Dark green olive above, shading to yellow lower on the flanks and white on the belly. The darker flanks are marked with numerous short, light colored horizontal bars. The fins have darker markings/spots. The fins are sometimes reddish. Northern pike have light on dark body coloring; muskellunge have the opposite.

Size: Most fish caught probably average between 5-10 pounds. But fish of twice that aren't uncommon. They can grow to around 50 pounds in the United States. Their European counterparts grow far larger. As northern pike grow larger they tend to get fatter rather than longer.

IGFA All-Tackle World Record 55 pound 1 ounce, Lake of Grefeern, Germany.

Tackle and fishing: A very aggressive fish that fights hard, jumps and runs when hooked. Baitcast, spin and fly tackle are productive on northern pike. They are easier to tempt onto the hook compared to the Muskellunge and tiger musky, and will eat virtually any live baitfish, lure or fly put in their path. They will cannibalise when other fish prey become scarce. They will hit a wide variety of lures, as per muskellunge, as well as large popping or streamer flies. They seem to be more attracted to brightly colored lures and flies than natural colored offerings.

Edibility: Very good. Flesh is white and mild tasting. In certain areas it is mandatory to kill a northern pike that are caught to stop them establishing outside their native range.

Game status: Exceptional.

PIKEMINNOW, COLORADO

Scientific name: Ptychocheilus lucius. Also known as Colorado squawfish, white salmon.

Range: Native to the Colorado River basin.. Threatened and endangered due to habitat alteration.

Habitat: Deep pools and eddies.

Description: Elongated body with a flattened and elongated cone shaped head. Coloration is olive green/gray above with yellow/silver flanks and white belly. Young fish have a dark spot on the caudal fin.

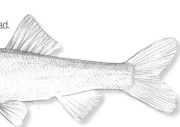

Size: The largest of the North American pikeminnows. Reports of fish in the past growing to 6 feet in length and 100 pounds in weight. Modern day fish rarely reach 15 inches.

Tackle and fishing: Most anglers avoid targeting due to its vulnerable status. A solid fighter for its size. Takes lures and various baits.

Edibility: Poor.

Game status: Very good. Avoid targeting to protect the species.

PIKEMINNOW, NORTHERN

Scientific name: Ptychocheilus oregonensis. Also known as common pikeminnow, northern squawfish, Columbia River dace, Columbia pikeminnow.

Range: British Columbia, Washington and Oregon. Coastal drainages in these states.

Habitat: Smaller fish mostly inhabit smaller streams and large fish the interior lakes. Deep, rocky holes, especially below dams. A voracious predator of salmon and steelhead eggs and smolt. Regarded as a pest by many salmon anglers.

Description: Back is dark green or green/brown with a cream/white belly area. Fins are clear but male fish can have orange/yellow lower fins during spawning periods. A longish head with small eyes, the tail is distinctly forked.

Similar to the other three pikeminnows in general appearance. Geographic location is the best distinguishing factor.

Size: Average weight would be 2-4 pounds but they can reach 25 pounds.

Tackle and fishing: A good fighter on light spin or baitcasting tackle using live minnows, bread, worms, roe, plugs, spoons and inline spinners. Jigging is also popular.

Edibility: Poor.

Game status: Good.

PIKEMINNOW, SACRAMENTO

Scientific name: Ptychocheilus grandis. Also known as Sacramento squawfish.

Range: Clear lake, Sacramento-San-Joaquin, Russian, Pajaro-Salinas and upper Pit River drainages. Illegally introduced into other Californian waters such as the Salt River.

Habitat: Clear low to mid-elevation rivers. Prefer deep pools and slow runs with rocky and sandy bottoms and plenty of aquatic vegetation and bankside cover. Also found in lakes.

Description: An elongated fish with a flattened head, large mouth and deeply forked tail. Coloration of larger fish is dark brown/olive or blue/gray/green above with gold/yellow or silver below.

Identification from other pikeminnows is often determined by geography.

Size: Mostly between 1-2 pounds.

Tackle and fishing: Not a great fighter, but a voracious feeder. Usually taken with poles or light spin tackle with baits such as worms, minnows and aquatic insects or small spoons and spinners etc.

Edibility: Poor.

Game status: Average.

PIKEMINNOW, UMPQUA

Scientific name: Ptychocheilus umpquae. Also known as Umpqua squawfish.

Range: Umpqua and Siuslaw River drainages in Oregon. Also Siltcoos, Woahink and Tahkentich Lakes in Oregon. Rogue River Oregon.

Habitat: Inhabits lakes and pools and sluggish to moderate flows in small rivers and creeks. Usually found in water less than 3 feet deep.

Description: The smallest of the pikeminnows. Similar in appearance to the northern pikeminnow.

Size: Rarely reaches 2 pounds in weight.

Tackle and fishing: Only an average fighting fish that is usually taken with spin tackle using live minnows or lures such as spoons, plugs and in line spinners.

Edibility: Poor.

Game status: Average.

PUMPKINSEED

Scientific name: Lepomis gibbosus. Also known as sunny, pond perch, common sunfish, punkys, sunfish.

Range: Natural range is from New Brunswick down to South Carolina. Across middle of North America, through Iowa and Pennsylvania. It has now been widely introduced across many areas of the United States.

Habitat: Throughout warm lakes and ponds and small creeks and rivers with plenty of vegetation. They predominantly hug the shoreline around shallow protected areas with structure such as weedbeds, docks, and boat ramps. They are active during the day and rest up around submerged logs etc at night. They travel in schools and are often found with bluegills.

Description: The body is a mixture of colors. Mostly olive green overall, with orange, yellow and blue markings. They have numerous spots and speckles over the flanks and back and a golden yellow/orange breast area. The flanks also feature vertical bars in a pale green or blue color. They have a distinct bright orange/red spot immediately behind the black patch on the gill cover.

Size: Typically 6-8 inches in length but can grow bigger. Most are 4-10 ounces in weight and rarely exceed 1 pound. The world record is 1 pound 6 ounces.

Tackle and fishing: A fun fish to catch (especially for children) but no great fighting abilities. Anglers using poles (or spin tackle) and worms catch the most fish, but spincasting lures and flyfishing are also productive and fun. They will hit small jigs and spinners, and wet and dry flies. Other baits include grubs and bread.

Edibility: Excellent. Excellent flavor, low in fat and high in protein.

Game status: Fun. Especially for kids as they feed throughout the day and are easily caught.

QUILLBACK

Scientific name: Carpiodes cyprinus. Also known as highfin, white sucker, white carp, broad mullet, quillback sucker, long-finned sucker.

Range: Most common carpsucker. Large rivers of Middle America. Great Lakes.

Habitat: Warm water, medium to large rivers and streams. Some lakes and impoundments. Shallow slow waters, backwaters, side channels and flats.

Description: A large, heavy bodied fish with a long, pointed dorsal fin that has a 'quill' that extends to the base of the dorsal. Coloration is overall silver or metallic gold depending on the environment. They have small, underslung mouths for sifting bottom dwelling food.

QUILLBACK CONTINUED...

Size: Most average around 2 pounds but can grow to about 10 pounds.

Tackle and fishing: A strong fighter if you're good enough to hook one! They are very difficult to catch using conventional tackle, anglers use very light gear with super small pieces of worm or dough on small hooks. They take the bait so lightly that anglers often use super sensitive quill floats or ledger rigs.

Edibility: Good.

Game status: Very good. On light tackle, especially in streams with deep, fast currents.

REDHORSE, BLACKTAIL

Scientific name: Moxostoma poecilurum.

Range: Throughout Mississippi tributaries from Southern Kentucky to Galveston Bay in Texas. Florida Panhandle and Mobile Delta.

Habitat: Commonly found in riffles and runs of small to medium sized rivers with rock, gravel, silt or sand bottoms. They hang around aquatic vegetation. Sometimes found in lakes and swamps.

Description: A long cylindrical body, the head blunt with a sub terminal mouth. Coloration is gray/olive or orange/brown dorsally with silver/golden brown flanks and white belly. Fins usually have some rust/reddish shading, especially the dorsal and upper lobe of the tail fin. The dorsal fin also has a black band at its tip. The lower section of the tail fin has a distinct black stripe, hence the name blacktail.

Size: Mostly between 10-16 inches in length.

Tackle and fishing: Its size restricts any real fight. Mostly taken with poles and light spin tackle using worms and other aquatic insects.

Edibility: Fair.

Game status: Fair.

REDHORSE, GOLDEN

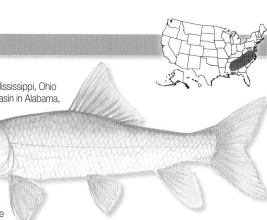

Scientific name: Moxostoma erythrurum.

Range: Across 25 eastern half states of North America. Mississippi, Ohio and Missouri River drainage basins. Mobile Bay drainage basin in Alabama, Georgia and Tennessee. Great Lakes (excluding Superior).

Habitat: Prefers calm, silty and sandy areas in small to large rivers, creeks, streams and lakes. Mostly a stream fish. Unlike other redhorse species, the golden redhorse isn't as sensitive to poor environmental conditions.

Description: Olive/bronze color with lighter sides, white belly and slate gray tail fins. Lower fins can have an orange tinge.

Size: Average 12-18 inches in length and between 1-2 pounds in weight. They can grow to 26 inches and 4-5 pounds.

Tackle and fishing: Puts up a reasonable fight on light tackle. Many are caught by anglers fishing the bottom for catfish. They will take worms and aquatic insect baits. Often speared at night from boats.

Edibility: Fair. Smoked or pickled.

Game status: Fair.

REDHORSE, RIVER

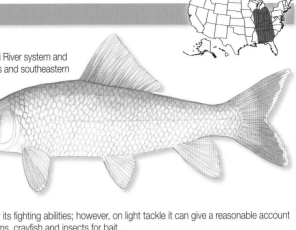

Scientific name: Moxostoma carinatum.

Range: Throughout central and eastern Mississippi River system and the Gulf slope from Florida to Louisiana. Great Lakes and southeastern Canada.

Habitat: Throughout central and eastern Mississippi River system and the Gulf slope from Florida to Louisiana. Great Lakes and south eastern Canada.

Description: A large flat head with a prominent snout, big eyes and a thick body. Bright red caudal and anal fins. Coloration is olive/gold above with silver flanks.

Size: From 2-10 pounds.

Tackle and fishing: Perhaps not recognised for its fighting abilities; however, on light tackle it can give a reasonable account of itself. Most are taken on bottom gear using worms, crayfish and insects for bait.

Edibility: Fair.

Game status: Good.

REDHORSE, SHORTHEAD

Scientific name: Moxostoma macrolepidotum. Also known as northern redhorse, redfin redhorse, sucker.

Range: A wide-ranging species in North America. Great Lakes and Mississippi River drainages to Arkansas and Tennessee. New York to South Carolina. Canada.

Very sensitive to pollutants.

Habitat: A wide range of habitats. Small to large rivers and lakes, preferably where there is gravel and sand bottoms. They feed in riffles and along riffle edges. They move into swift flowing water to spawn.

An important prey fish for larger predators such as muskellunge and northern pike.

Description: A small head and long slender body. Coloration is olive/brown dorsally with gold to silver sides and a bright red tail. Very similar to the smallmouth redhorse but longer in the body and with a concave dorsal fin.

Sometimes mistaken for carp, but shorthead redhorse are an indication of a healthy waterway, unlike carp.

Size: Most are 12-18 inches in length, but can grow to 25 inches. Usually 2-3 pounds but can achieve 6 pounds in weight.

Tackle and fishing: A moderately good fighting fish that is taken with natural insect baits and worms etc. fished on the bottom, using poles, spin or baitcasting tackle.

Edibility: Good.

Game status: Good.

SAILFIN MOLLY

Scientific name: Poecilia latipinna. Also known as tabai.

Range: North Carolina to Texas and the Yucatan Peninsula of Mexico. Very common in Florida.

Habitat: Fresh, brackish and coastal saltwater in lowland habitats. Ponds, swamps, ditches and marshes close to floating vegetation and other in-water structure.

Capable of exploiting oxygen poor environments.

Description: A small head with a small upturned mouth. A very large, rounded caudal fin and caudal peduncle. The dorsal fin is very large also, especially in mature males. Body coloration is usually a light gray/green with rows of darker spots running along the body creating the appearance of stripes.

Size: Can grow to around 6 inches in length.

Tackle and fishing: A prized aquarium fish that has no value for recreational anglers other than as bait for popular fish such as crappie, sunfish and bass.

Edibility: N/A.

Game status: N/A.

SALMON, ATLANTIC

Scientific name: Also known as Sebago salmon, kelt, black salmon, kennebec salmon, bay salmon, ouananiche.

Range: Northern Atlantic Ocean and rivers that flow into the north Atlantic. Atlantic provinces of Canada. A few rivers of Maine. Landlocked populations in the Great Lakes.

Habitat: Although some populations of landlocked Atlantic salmon never go to sea, for the most part, Atlantic salmon is anadromous. For the most part they live and grow at sea before returning to their birth stream to spawn. They do not have to go to saltwater to survive and spawn however.

Description: A large salmon. Similar in body shape to other salmonoids. Sea run fish are bright silver with small black crosses/spots predominantly along the upper flanks and sides. They are blue/black dorsally. Spawning males in freshwater take on a brown and red spotted mottled coloring and feature a very pronounced kype or hooked lower jaw.

Size: Can grow to 100 pound and 60 inches in length. Size depends on age and their environment. Large sea run river fish often reach 30 pounds while younger Grilse average 2-8 pound. Fish that have been at sea for two years generally weigh between 8-12 pounds.

IGFA All-Tackle World Record 79 pound 2 ounces, Tana River, Norway.

Tackle and fishing: A spectacular fighting sportfish that leaps high, runs hard and strong. The pinnacle of freshwater sportfish for most freshwater anglers. They are generally targeted by fly fishers using 'salmon' flies in rivers. They will hit spoons, spinners and other lures that are trolled or cast in rivers, lakes and estuaries. They will also take natural baits such as live baitfish, shrimp, worms and various aquatic baits. Sea run spawning fish stop feeding once they enter rivers but will hit flies and lures swum past their noses out of aggression. Landlocked fish feed normally before spawning.

Edibility: Excellent. One of the finest eating fish worldwide.

Game status: Excellent.

SALMON, CHINOOK

Scientific name: Oncorhynchus tshawytscha. Also known as king salmon, quinnat salmon, blackmouth, spring salmon, tyee.

Range: Bering Strait area off Alaska, to Southern California. Introduced into all of the Great Lakes as well as other lakes in other states. Landlocked fish do not naturally reproduce and these fisheries are therefore reliant on stocking to maintain the fishery.

Habitat: Anadromous species. Juvenile fish spend from 3 months to two years in the stream they were born before heading first to estuarine areas and then to sea as adults. Adults spend between 1-6 years (normally 2-4 years) at sea before returning to spawn in their birth stream, and then die.

Description: In the sea and the Great Lakes, fish are blue/green dorsally, darker blue on back, and with silver sides. Numerous small black dots on the body above the lateral line, and on both lobes of the tail. Distinct black pigmenting inside of the mouth along the base of the teeth. This is a distinguishing identifier from other salmon.

Similar to coho salmon (Oncorhynchus kisutch) when taken from the sea.

Size: Largest of the Pacific salmon. Can grow to 120 pounds but usually from 10-20 pounds with 40 pounders not uncommon. They mature at 36 inches and 30 pounds in weight.

IGFA All-Tackle World Record 97pounds 4 ounces, Kenai River, AK, USA.

Tackle and fishing: A mighty and strong fighting fish, deserving of the name 'king'. Most Pacific anglers concentrate their efforts on catching these fish when they enter bays and estuaries on the spawning runs. Strong spin, baitcast and light saltwater tackle are employed, often trolling deep plugs and spoons, or live and dead fish baits behind flashers and dodgers to attract the fish's attention.

Casting lures such as spoons and spinners, and streamer or egg pattern flies in stream mouths and further upstream is effective.

Edibility: Excellent. Fresh or smoked.

Game status: Exceptional.

SALMON, CHUM

Scientific name: Oncorhynchus keta. Also known as dog salmon, fall salmon, calico salmon.

Range: Most widely distributed of all the Pacific salmon. Alaska to Northern California.

Habitat: Estuaries and lower reaches of rivers during their return to spawn in fall. Some fish do travel far upstream but the majority spawn in the lower reaches. Most of their lives are spent at sea, similar to other Pacific salmon.

Description: Anadromous species. Ocean fish are metallic blue/green on the back and down to the lateral line,and silver below. They have numerous small black speckles or spots but not as pronounced as those on Chinook, pink and Coho salmon. The tail is heavily forked and not spotted. When adult male and female chum salmon enter freshwater on their spawning run their appearance changes dramatically. Male fish become dark olive-brown with red to purple wavy vertical stripes along the body and develop a pronounced kype (hooked lower jaw) filled with canine-like teeth. The females become brown/gray with a broad, dark horizontal bar running along the flank. They also develop a smaller kype and canine-like teeth, hence the name 'dog salmon'. They spawn once,and then die.

Size: Chum salmon quickly grow to around 10-13 pounds or more during their 3-4 years at sea. Males are usually larger than females. Maximum weight is around 35 pounds with 20-25 pounders reasonably common. IGFA All-Tackle World Record 35 pound, Edye Pass, British Columbia.

Tackle and fishing: A solid fighting fish when taken early on during their spawning aggregation. Once they start to turn color they start to deteriorate. Usually targeted on spin or fly tackle. Small spoons and spinners work well for lure anglers, whilefly anglers prefer streamer flies and shrimp patterns.

Edibility: Good. Not as popular as other Pacific salmon. Better if caught and eaten before they turn color on their spawning run.

Game status: Very good. Not as flashy as other salmon.

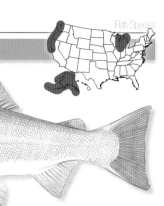

SALMON, COHO

Scientific name: Oncorhynchus kisutch. Also known as silver salmon, blueback.

Range: Bering Sea to mainland Alaska, south to Monterey Bay, California. Introduced into the Great Lakes and other landlocked reservoirs across the United States.

Habitat: Andromous species. Along the Pacific coast and the Great Lakes. Enter their birth streams from July to November and although they do not feed once they begin their spawning runs, they can be tempted to strike lures and flies. The young spend one to three winters in streams and up to five winters in lakes before migrating to sea as smolt. They die after spawning.

Description: Sea fish or fish recently returned to freshwater are bright silver with steel/ metallic blue or greenish backs and whitish bellies. They have small black spots on their back and upper lobe of the tail fin. Theirgums are white unlike Chinook salmon (Oncorhynchus tshawytscha) that have black gums and spots on the upper and lower tail fin lobes.

Spawning adults of both sexes have darker (olive) backs and upper head, and maroon or red over the whole body and dorsal, anal and caudal fins.

Size: Adults normally weigh between 8-12 pounds and reach 24 – 30 inches in length. They can grow to just over 30 pounds.

IGFA All-Tackle World Record 33 pound 4 ounces, Salmon River, Pulaski, NY, USA.

Tackle and fishing: A great fighter, that leaps and performs strong speedy runs when hooked. Mostly targeted trolling deep with heavy rods and large spoons, plugs and rigged live baitfish or fillets. They will hit cast lures and flies on lighter tackle when they are within reach and near the surface in bays, estuaries and rivers. They like flashy metallic spinners and streamer flies.

They are also targeted by angler's drift fishing and using live or dead baitfish.

Edibility: Excellent. Fresh or smoked.

Game status: Excellent. One of the best.

SALMON, KOKANEE (LANDLOCKED SOCKEYE SALMON)

Scientific name: Oncorhynchus nerka. Also known as landlocked sockeye, silver trout.

Range: Completely landlocked populations of sockeye salmon (kokonee) live (and spawn) in lakes, and others that live in lakes and reproduce in any inflowing streams. These landlocked populations exist in British Columbia in Canada, Alaska, Washington, Oregon, California, New York, Utah, Idaho, Montana, Nevada, New Mexico and Wyoming.

Habitat: Throughout the whole water column in lakes feeding on zooplankton.

Description: They are the same as the sea going sockeye salmon. Blue backs with silver bodies and small black dots back and tail. Breeding fish change colour similar to the anadromous sockeye. Like the anadromous fish, landlocked fish also die after spawning.

Size: Much smaller than the sea going anadromous sockeye. Rarely greater than 14 inches in length. Can grow to around 20 inches.

IGFA All-Tackle World Record 9 pound 6 ounces, Okanagan Lake, British Columbia.

Tackle and fishing: Their small size dictates the use of ultralight tackle. They have soft mouths so rods should be soft in action. They put up a good tussle on such gear. Despite being plankton feeders, they will hit small flashy spinners or spoons tipped with small pieces of worm. Anglers trolling strings of dodgers or blades ahead of these lures take most fish. Other anglers use baits including aquatic insects, corn, worms, salmon eggs fished on size 12-8 sized hooks.

Jigging with ¼ to 1 oz. jigs is effective when large schools are located.

Edibility: Excellent.

Game status: Very good.

SALMON, PINK

Scientific name: Oncorhynchus gorbuscha. Also known as Humpie, humpback salmon.

Range: Pacific and Arctic coastal waters. Mackenzie River in Canada down to the Sacramento River California. Introduced into the Great Lakes.

Pink salmon are more abundant in northern waters in even numbered years and in southern waters in odd numbered years.

Habitat: Mostly targeted in the lower rivers and estuaries and lakes. They return to rivers to reproduce as two-year-old adults spawn and then die.

Pink and Chum salmon sometimes hybridize and their sterile offspring are called miko salmon. So do pink and Chinook salmon in Lake Michigan and their offspring are called pinooks.

Description: Ocean going fish are bright silver with metallic blue backs. They have numerous black spots on the back and tails. Once they return to rivers to spawn their coloring changes to a pale gray/brown on the back with yellow/white belly. Sometimes spawning fish take on an overall dull green coloration. They have a white mouth and black gums and no teeth on the tongue.

During spawning, males develop a pronounced hump back.

Size: The smallest of all the salmon species. Average 3-5 pounds. Maximum 15 pounds.

IGFA All-Tackle World Record 14 pound 13 ounces, Monroe, WA.

Tackle and fishing: A tough and strong sportfish that is better suited to lighter tackle due to its smaller size. They are aggressive feeders and will hit various flashy lures and flies with gusto.

Edibility: Good. Flesh is pink. Good when smoked or canned.

Game status: Good.

SALMON, SOCKEYE

Scientific name: Oncorhynchus nerka. Also known as kokanee salmon, blueback salmon, red salmon.

Range: Northern Pacific Ocean and the rivers flowing into it. Arctic Alaska south to the Columbia River in Oregon/Washington. Occasionally down into California.

Habitat: An anadromous fish that spends two/three years in the ocean before returning to freshwater rivers to spawn and then die. Fished for in estuaries and rivers where they spawn.

Description: Fish living in, or immediately from the salt have a bluish back over a silver colored body and tiny black spots on the tail and upper body. As they progress upstream to spawn their coloring changes dramatically. Their body becomes a bright red, their head and tail turn olive green. The mouth area takes on a black tinge. Females are similar in coloring but duller.

Size: Mostly between 5-8 pounds. Can grow to around twice that weight.

IGFA All-Tackle World Record 15 pound 3 ounces, Kenai River, AK.

Tackle and fishing: Not the best of the salmon, but a great fighter none the less. The angling environment usually determines the type and strength of tackle being used. In estuaries and big brawling rivers anglers tend to use stouter spin and baitcasting tackle, while once the fish have moved further upriver, lighter spin and fly tackle come into their own. Once they have moved upstream to spawn they stop feeding and anglers need to elicit aggressive territorial strikes.

Before the fish run upriver, they are trolled for in the estuaries and large downstream river mouths down deep with large flies and flashy lures.

Edibility: Exceptional. Flesh is very red.

Game status: Excellent.

SCULPIN, FOURHORN

Scientific name: Myoxocephalus quadricornis or Triglopsis quadricornis. Also known as scorpion fish.

Range: Northern Arctic Ocean areas and freshwater environments of the extreme north.

Habitat: Brackish Arctic coastal waters near the shore in both streams and lakes.

Description: The sea-going form has four bony protuberances that are absent in the landlocked freshwater form of the species. It has no swim bladder so it is a true bottom dweller.

A large knobbly head with protruding lips. Upper body is mottled dark brown. The belly is creamy/yellow/white.

Size: Sea fish grow between 8-12 inches. Freshwater forms rarely exceed 6 inches.

Tackle and fishing: Not targeted by recreational anglers but can be caught on small bottom baits, spinners and wet flies.

Edibility: N/A.

Game status: N/A.

SCULPIN, MOTTLED

Scientific name: Cottus bairdi. Also known as gudgeon, Columbia sculpin, miller's thumb.

Range: Widespread, but not continuous in areas of the United States, including the Tennessee River, Missouri River, the Bonneville system of Great Basin and the Columbia River in Canada. Mountainous states from Colorado to Washington.

Habitat: Well-oxygenated fast current areas and riffles in cool, clear small streams, springs and rocky lake shores.

They are predated on by trout and other sportfish.

Description: Eyes at the top of the head and a relatively large mouth. They have no scales on the body.

Back and sides are made up of a mixture of brown, gray and black mottling. They have 3-4 darker saddles over their back and down the sides and a dark vertical bar at the tail. Belly area is a light cream color. A large pectoral fin that is banded.

Spawning males have a red outer edge on the first small dorsal fin.

Size: Typically 2-4 inches in length but they can grow to 5 inches.

Tackle and fishing: Not specifically targeted by anglers but do make good bait. They can be caught with hook and line using small worm baits and wet flies.

Edibility: N/A.

Game status: N/A. Good for bait.

SCULPIN, SLIMY

Scientific name: Cottus cognatus. Also known as northern sculpin, slimy muddler, Columbia slimy sculpin.

Range: Along much of the Arctic coast in Alaska and Canada. Broadly distributed in Northern America.

Habitat: Cool water streams and lakes over pebble and rubble substrates.

Description: Not slimy as the name suggests. A flat wide head with eyes on top so typical with sculpins. Dark brown and mottled above fading to cream/white on the underside. The first dorsal fin is very dark at the base and other fins have light barring. There are no scales on the body.

Size: Usually 2-3 inches but can reach 5 inches.

Tackle and fishing: Not targeted by anglers. Sometimes taken with wet flies or small baits. It is a prime forange fish for larger sportfish.

Edibility: N/A.

Game status: N/A.

SEATROUT, SPOTTED

Scientific name: Cynoscion nebulosus. Also known as seatrout, speckled seatrout, spotted weakfish, speck.

Range: Limited to the Western Atlantic Ocean. Cape Cod to southern Florida and the Gulf of Mexico.

Habitat: Shallow coastal and estuarine waters through to deeper Gulf waters and bays at times. Tidal pools and salt marshes, surf beaches and coastal streams, moving about following food supplies. They reside in salt marshes and tidal pools and channels, and are usually associated with seagrass beds and sandy-bottomed areas. Often head up into freshwater rivers when the weather turns cold.

Description: Body is very silvery with numerous irregular dark spots on the upper back from the dorsal fin back and including the tail fin. The upper body background color is dark gray/blue with the lower sides and belly silver. The dorsal fins and tail show a yellow tinge. The large mouth contains prominent canine teeth.

Similar to the Weakfish in appearance except for the seatrouts numerous prominent spots.

Size: Typically caught around the 1-2 pound mark although fish to 4 pound aren't uncommon. Maximum weight is around 18 pound.

IGFA All-Tackle World Record 17 pound 7 ounces Ft.Pierce, FL, USA.

Tackle and fishing: Not renowned for their fighting abilities although they do strike hard. They are more splashy fighters with the occasional leap rather than speedsters.

Best targeted using light tackle to get the best fight, with spin, baitcasting and fly gear all being effective. Casting soft plastic baits and jigs, top and submerged plugs or large, flashy streamers and surface poppers (in shallower waters) on fly outfits. Natural baits such as live or dead shrimp, small live baitfish, plus cut baits of fish or squid etc.

Edibility: Very good.

Game status: Good. Best on light tackle.

SHAD, ALABAMA

Scientific name: Alosa alabamae. Also known as Ohio shad.

Range: Gulf coast drainages. Mississippi River to the Suwannee River.

Habitat: Adults live in saltwater and spawn in medium/large flowing rivers from the above river drainages. In some Gulf coast drainages. Sometimes in or around river mouths.

The population of this fish has significantly declined over the past decades in a large part due to the construction of dams stopping the fish reaching traditional spawning grounds.

Description: Mostly silver in color with greenish/purple sheen dorsally. Distinguished by a distinct median notch in its upper jaw. A single dark spot behind the gill cover. Closely resemble skipjack herring and the American shad to which it is closely related.

Size: Can grow to 18 inches in length. Averages around one pound in weight.

Tackle and fishing: Solid fighters when caught on light spin or fly tackle. Will hit cast or trolled spoons, jigs and flies.

Edibility: Good.

Game status: Very good. On light tackle.

SHAD, AMERICAN

Scientific name: Alosa sapidissima. Also known as common shad, white shad, Atlantic shad.

Range: Nova Scotia to the St.Johns River, Florida.

Habitat: An anadromous fish that spends most of its life (4-5 years) at sea in large schools before returning to freshwater to spawn. They return to the ocean after spawning.

Description: Largest of the river herring family.

Color is green above with silver flanks and belly. A large and prominent dark spot on the shoulder often trailing off with several faint spots. Has sharp 'saw like' scales running along the belly. The lower jaw does not extend past the upper jaw.

Size: The largest of the shads growing to 30 inches. Most are caught between 2-4 pounds with fish to 5 pounds common.

IGFA All-Tackle World Record 11 pound 4 ounces, Conn. River, S. Hadley, MA, USA.

Tackle and fishing: A wonderful fighting fish, that leaps and offers a great fight. The majority are taken on light bait or spincasting tackle but they are also popular with fly anglers. Colored lead head jigs with grub tails, shad darts, spoons, micro-jigs and small minnow imitation lures are popular. Flyfishing with gold and white soft-bodied streamers.

Edibility: Good. Bony.

Game status: Excellent.

SHAD, GIZZARD

Scientific name: Dorosoma cepedianum. Also known as shad, herring, skipjack, hickory shad.

Range: Native to eastern North America. Saint Lawrence River and Great Lakes, west to North Dakota. South as far as Mexico and west to New Mexico.

Habitat: Large rivers and reservoirs. In large schools.

Description: Easily distinguished from the Threadfin shad by its projecting upper jaw and lack of yellow color in the fins. Silver body with silver/blue above and almost white on the lower flanks and belly.

Size: Commonly grows to 9-14 inches in length and can exceed 20 inches on rare occasions.

IGFA All-Tackle World Record 4 pound 6 ounces, Lake Michigan, IN, USA.

Tackle and fishing: A fish used as cut bait for larger sporting species. They rarely bite on baits. Most are caught in nets.

Edibility: N/A. Used as bait.

Game status: N/A. Used as bait.

SHAD, HICKORY

Scientific name: Alosa mediocris. Also known as fall herring, hickory, silver shad.

Range: Gulf of Maine to Florida along the east coast.

Habitat: A schooling anadromous species that inhabits the near shore coast and enter estuaries and freshwater rivers to spawn during spring.

Description: Similar in appearance to American shad. Silver sided with gray/green back and a prominent dark spot at the rear of the gill cover followed by a horizontal row of lighter spots. A protruding lower jaw.

Size: Average 1 pound with fish around 2 pounds not uncommon.

Tackle and fishing: A flashy fighter that often tail walks and leaps when hooked. Often arrive earlier on their spawning runs than American shad do. Light spin tackle using very small, spoons, jigs, swimming minnows or live minnow baits. Fly anglers using streamers and other wet flies.

Edibility: Very good. Very bony though.

Game status: Very good. On light tackle.

SHAD, THREADFIN

Scientific name: Dorosoma petenense.

Range: Transplanted to waters across most of the United States. Mostly the south eastern United States.

Habitat: A schooling fish in large rivers and lakes. Often seen feeding on the surface, and often in company with gizzard shad. They are attracted to light and can be found around lit up docks at night.

Description: The elongated ray at the end of the dorsal fin is where it gets its name. Gizzard shad have a similar feature. Coloration is bluish gray/green dorsally with lower sides silver/creamy white. Caudal fin is often a yellowish tint. A prominent black or purple spot immediately behind the gill plate. It has a pointed snout and front opening mouth unlike the similar in appearance gizzard shad.

Size: Grows from 5-7 inches in length.

Tackle and fishing: A plankton feeder and as such rarely caught on hook and line. They provide good bait for larger sportfish and are usually caught with nets.

Edibility: N/A. Used as bait.

Game status: N/A. Used as bait.

SHARK, BULL

Scientific name: Carcharhinus leucas. Also known as cub shark, river shark, ground shark.

Range: All Florida coasts, entire Gulf of Mexico, Bahamas, Caribbean and as far north as Massachusetts.

Habitat: Prefers coastal waters less than 100 feet deep primarily along beaches, bays, harbors, lagoons, tidal rivers and often far upstream in freshwater rivers.

Description: Very solid looking body with a blunt snout, hence the name. They have small eyes. Coloring is dark to light gray dorsally and upper flanks fading to white below. Young fish have black tipped fins, which fade with age.

Size: Grow to 11.5 feet and 500 pounds. Most common around 5-8 feet in length and around 100-300 pounds in weight.

Tackle and fishing: A solid fighting fish due to its size. It is popular with recreational anglers fishing from shore, beaches, piers and bridges as well as those fishing the flats. Its large size often dictates that it should be fished with heavier ocean tackle but sportfishers often target this shark with spin, plug and fly tackle. It will readily take a range of live and dead cut baits and can be chummed closer to anglers casting lures or flies.

Edibility: Good.

Game status: Excellent. Especially when taken on Sportfishing tackle.

SHEEPSHEAD

Scientific name: Archosargus probatocephalus. Also known as Convict fish, pargo, sargo.

Range: Nova Scotia south to and throughout the Gulf of Mexico. Greatest numbers off southwest Florida.

Habitat: Mostly inshore around jetties, piers, rock pilings and tidal creeks. Offshore in late winter early spring for spawning. Young fish found over seagrass flats and mud bottom areas. Brackish water in river mouths, estuaries and tidal creeks. Moves into freshwater also.

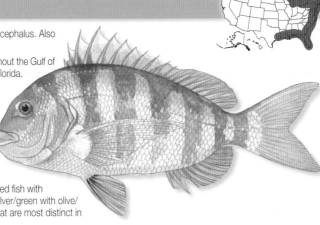

Description: A deep-bodied, oval shaped fish with numerous protruding fish. Adult fish are silver/green with olive/gray back. Five or six dark vertical bars that are most distinct in young fish.

Size: Mostly caught from 1-5 pound with fish around 7 pound still plentiful. Maximum size is around 22 pound.

Tackle and fishing: A tough fighter on light tackle. Light spin, saltwater and baitcasting outfits with enough stiffness to set the hook into the fish's tough mouth are suitable. Primarily feed on blue crab, oysters, clams and other crustaceans and these baits are all suitable when targeting these fish. Live and dead shrimp, sand fleas and small crabs are also popular bait. Slowly worked jigs will catch these fish at times.

Edibility: Excellent.

Game status: Good. On light tackle.

SHINER, EMERALD

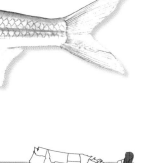

Scientific name: Notropis atherinoides. Also known as lake shiner, plains shiner.

Range: From Canada to the Gulf of Mexico. Great Lakes.

Habitat: Large, deep lakes and medium to wide rivers. Most common over sand or gravel substrate. Occasionally in smaller waters also.

Description: Overall silver with an iridescent light green back. Has an emerald green stripe along the flanks. Large eyes. A slender flat-sided fish.

Size: Grow to approximately 4 inches.

Tackle and fishing: A popular baitfish. Normally caught in nets by anglers hunting bait.

Edibility: N/A.

Game status: N/A.

SHINER, GOLDEN

Scientific name: Notemigonus crysoleucas. Also known as roach, bitterhead chub.

Range: Native to eastern half of North America. It has been transplanted widely in the west because of its common use as bait. A common pond-cultured fish in the United States.

Habitat: In a variety of habitats. They prefer quite waters mostly in ponds, sloughs, ditches and lakes. Sometimes found in quite areas of streams. They are tolerant of pollution and prefer weedy areas. They live in large groups.

Description: A deep-bodied fish with a dark green/olive back and silvery/white belly. Larger fish tend to be golden color on the flanks. Sometimes with a dusky stripe along the sides. A small, upturned mouth and yellowish fins.

Size: Can reach 12 inches but generally 3-5 inches long in the wild.

Tackle and fishing: A popular baitfish that is easily caught. A popular fish for young anglers to catch. They will take worms, dough, and bread and can be chummed to an area. Poles and light spin gear are popular but many are caught using nets by anglers chasing bait.

Edibility: Poor.

Game status: Poor. Popular for bait.

SHINER, RIVER

Scientific name: Notropis blennius.

Range: Hudson Bay basin to Manitoba to Alberta, Canada and south to Minnesota and North Dakota. Mississippi River basin from Wisconsin and Minnesota south to the Gulf.

Habitat: Pools and main channels of medium to large rivers over silt, sand and gravel substrates.

Description: Darker tan/olive above with silver sides. A distinct darker stripe along the upper back that encircles the base of the dorsal fin. All fins are transparent. A large mouth and small eyes.

Size: Normally 3-4 inches but can reach 5 inches in length.

Tackle and fishing: A valuable baitfish that can be taken with nets.

Edibility: N/A.

Game status: N/A. Used as bait.

Fish Species

SILVERSIDE, ATLANTIC

Scientific name: Menidia menidia. Also known as sand smelt, glass minnow, shiner, spearing, rainfish.

Range: Bermuda. Gulf of St.Lawrence to Florida.

Habitat: In large schools in shallow water along sandy or gravel shoreline, rarely in deep water. In brackish estuaries and saltwater river mouths and sometimes further upstream into freshwater.

Description: A long slender fish with two dorsal fins. Color is light translucent olive/gray above, lighter below with a rounded white belly and silver band outlined with a thin black stripe along the flank running from the pectoral to caudal fin. Dark speckles along upper sides. A small mouth. Large scales on body.

Similar in appearance to other small baitfish.

Size: Can grow to 5-6 inches but usually between 2-4 inches in length.

Tackle and fishing: No recreational angling benefits. Taken in nets for bait by anglers chasing sportfish.

Edibility: Good. Rarely eaten but used for bait.

Game status: N/A.

SILVERSIDE, BROOK

Scientific name: Labidesthes sicculus. Also known as silverside.

Range: The Great Lakes to the Mississippi Basin and Gulf Coastal plains. Widely introduced as a forange fish for larger sportfish. Found in 27 U.S. states and Canada.

Habitat: Slow flowing freshwater rivers, ponds and lakes with clear water and good aquatic vegetation. A schooling fish of open water areas.

Description: A small, slender translucent fish with a long mouth that forms a pointed beak. Coloration is pale green or olive with a transparent body and silver stripe along the flanks.

Size: Usually 2-3 inches but can reach 4.5 inches in length.

Tackle and fishing: No recreational angling or eating qualities. This fish is good bait for larger sportfish and can be caught using nets where legal.

Edibility: N/A.

Game status: N/A. Good for bait.

SILVERSIDE, INLAND

Scientific name: Menidia beryllina. Also known as silverside.

Range: Widespread along the Atlantic coast from Maine to Florida. Along the Gulf of Mexico and the Mississippi River as far north as Illinois and Missouri. Introduced into California.

Habitat: Estuaries and far inland in freshwater.

Description: An elongate species with a flattened head, large eyes and upturned mouth. Two dorsal fins. Coloring is yellowish/olive above with bright silver sides and translucent olive/green belly area.

Size: Mostly between 3-4 inches in length.

Tackle and fishing: Taken with nets and used as bait. No recreational fishing benefits otherwise.

Edibility: N/A.

Game status: N/A.

SLEEPER, BIGMOUTH

Scientific name: Gobiomorus dormitor. Also known as rock bass.

Range: Southern Florida and southern Texas, USA to eastern Brazil. Islands of the Caribbean.

Habitat: Adults found in freshwater, often some distance inland in large clear, slower flowing streams. They hug the bottom around logs, large rocks and around gravel or leaf debris.

Description: Long bodied fish with a rounded, stout body and broad head. A large mouth with several rows of small conical teeth, two dorsal fins and rounded caudal fin. Coloring is a dull light or darker brown/olive above and on sides and whitish belly.

Size: Can grow to 24 inches in length. Most caught average 1 pound.

Tackle and fishing: Not a recognised fighter and usually taken as an accidental by-catch when anglers are chasing bass or snook with lures and jigs.

Edibility: Very good. Rarely targeted.

Game status: Poor.

SMELT, LONGFIN

Scientific name: Spirinchus thaleichthys. Also known as Sacramento smelt.

Range: Cook Inlet in Alaska south to the San Francisco Bay-Delta in California. Coastal drainage streams and some landlocked lakes.

Habitat: A pelagic estuarine fish found in bays and river mouths.

Description: The very long pectoral fins are a distinguishing feature. These fins reach almost right back to the pelvic fins. Coloring is olive/brown/pink iridescent above with silver sides. A long upper jaw and a slightly longer projecting lower jaw.

Size: To around 6 inches in length.

Tackle and fishing: Sometimes caught on small cut baits, but mostly taken with dip nets.

Edibility: Excellent.

Game status: N/A.

SMELT, RAINBOW

Scientific name: Osmerus mordax. Also known as Arctic smelt, American smelt, Atlantic smelt, pygmy smelt.

Range: Widespread across North American watersheds. In the Atlantic drainages from the Arctic to New Jersey, including the Great Lakes. As far south as Vancouver down the Pacific coast drainages. Introduced into waters across many U.S. states.

Habitat: Anadromous species that spends most of its life at sea before migrating up rivers to spawn. They prefer clear water along the edges of lakes. The building of dams has had an impact on their ability to move upstream and spawn in many locations.

Description: A slim and cylindrical body. Coloring is pale olive green/brown dorsally with silver flanks that have iridescent purple/blue/pink sheen. Belly is lighter. They often have a distinct bright silver band running along the flank.

Size: Grow between 7-9 inches in length mostly, and weigh 3 ounces, but can reach 12 inches.

Tackle and fishing: A commercially fished for species. They are also a popular winter recreational species, often taken by ice fishermen in rivers using small cut baits, worms etc. They are often taken in nets along lakeshores, and with dip nets, poles or very light spin tackle.

Edibility: Very good. When kept fresh.

Game status: N/A. Popular but not for their fight.

SNAKEHEAD, CHEVRON

Scientific name: Channa striata. Also known as snakehead, common snakehead, striped snakehead, banded snake head.

Range: Native to Southeast Asia. Hawaii. Potentially many areas where illegal releases are done into suitable habitats.

Habitat: Flooded fields in Asia. Shallow grassy vegetated areas.

Description: Slender long body with a head similar to a snake. Single long dorsal and anal fins. Sharp teeth. Coloration is mottled dark brown/black with paler sides and cream/yellow below. Feint dark bands along the length of the body.

Size: Usually around 1-3 pounds.

Tackle and fishing: No heavy weight fighter. Mostly taken on spin and baitcast tackle with live fish, cut baits and other natural baits. Will hit various lures such as spinners, plugs and spoons.

Edibility: Good. A delicacy in many Asian dishes.

Game status: Average.

SNAPPER, GRAY

Scientific name: Lutjanus griseus. Also known as Black snapper, mangrove snapper, gray silk, mango snapper, caballerote.

Range: Massachusetts to Bermuda. Bahamas, Gulf of Mexico and Caribbean Sea.

Habitat: From very shallow waters to depths of 585 feet. Often in large numbers over coral reefs, rocky habitats and estuaries. Juvenile fish live inshore around seagrass beds and a variety of other habitats. Both adults and juveniles have been found in freshwater lakes and rivers in south Florida. Adult fish usually frequent deeper waters around reefs, both coral and artificial and wrecks but can also be found in deeper channels and gutters.

Description: A relatively slender bodied fish that can be confused with young cubera snapper. They have pointed snouts and a large mouth and coloring can vary, although they are generally gray/green with a reddish tinge overall. Some small reddish to orange spots are evident along the sides. Young fish have a dark stripe running through the eye from the snout to the just below the dorsal fin and a less obvious blue stripe on the cheek below the eye.

Size: One of the smallest snappers and most young fish caught close to shore are rarely bigger than 12 inches. Fish caught offshore average 2-5 pound and almost always less than 10 pound.

Tackle and fishing: A strong fighting fish on appropriate tackle. The most successful tackle for these fish is light baitcasting, spin fishing and inshore boat tackle using live shrimp, live minnows, cut baits such as squid, shrimp and baitfish. Heavier offshore tackle such as spin, baitcasting and lighter offshore outfits are useful using cut baits. Inshore gray snapper will take lures and flies such as surface popper flies, plugs, jigs and streamers.

Edibility: Excellent.

Game status: Excellent. On appropriate tackle.

SNOOK, COMMON

Scientific name: Centropomus undecimalis. Also known as lineside, ravillia, robalo, saltwater pike, sergeant fish.

Range: Tropical Gulf waters of Mexico and the lower Gulf coast in Texas.

Habitat: Inlets, passes, underwater structure and pilings, docks and bridges, piers, surf and rivers not far from saltwater. Juvenile fish are mostly restricted to rivers and estuaries.

Description: The most common of the snook species.

Common snook have a slender body, a concave tapered snout, large mouth and jutting lower jaw. Body coloring is silver sides with dark gray, brown or black backs, white belly and distinct black lateral line. The two dorsal fins are quite well separated. Fins are generally yellowish.

Size: The largest of the Snooks. Average size is 3-15 pounds with fish to 30 pound common. They can grow to around 55-60 pounds in weight.

Tackle and fishing: One of the best all-round fighting fish. It usually executes long runs and full body lifting leaps in smaller fish, and half body lifts in big female fish. They will endeavour to wraps anglers lines around every likely snag when hooked.

Light boat rods with live bait through channels and inlets. Slightly heavier tackle when fishing from docks, bridges and piers. Usually targeted using baitcasters and medium-weight spinning tackle using a variety of bucktail and plastic jigs, spoons, jerk-baits, topwater and swimming plugs. Small live baits are very popular as are shrimp and crab baits, and large dead fish baits are popular for big fish. Chumming and baiting with pilchards is successful. Flyfishing with poppers and streamers also takes these fish.

Edibility: Excellent.

Game status: Excellent.

SNOOK, SWORDSPINE

Scientific name: Centropomus ensiferus. Also known as little snook.

Range: Rarest of the snooks. South Florida and Caribbean.

Habitat: Occurs along shoreline estuarine habitats, freshwater ponds and canals. Prefers only slightly brackish or freshwater.

Description: Smallest of all snooks. Most distinguishing feature from other snook is the extended length of the second anal fin spine. When folded back, this spine reaches past the beginning of the caudal fin. Color is generally yellow/green to brown/green above and silver below. Body scales are largest of all snook.

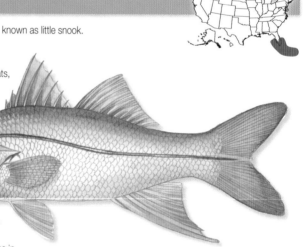

Size: Full-grown adults are less than twelve inches in length.

Tackle and fishing: A spirited striker and fighting fish for its diminutive size when caught on ultra light tackle. Best when targeted using ultra light spin, fly or baitcasting tackle using small jigs and flies. Can be caught using live shrimp bait.

Edibility: N/A. Too small.

Game status: Good. For its size.

SNOOK, TARPON

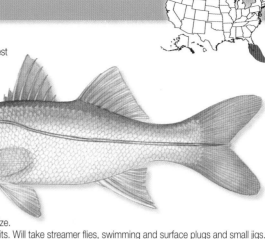

Scientific name: Centropomus pectinatus.

Range: South Florida and the Keys. Rare on Florida's west coast.

Habitat: Inshore, around mangrove areas, canals and ponds. Frequently in freshwater.

Description: Body is more compressed and thinner than other snooks. Head resembles that of Tarpon, hence the name, and colouring is similar to other snook. Prominent black lateral line that extends through the tail.

Size: Maximum size around 16-18 inches.

Tackle and fishing: Offers a reasonable fight for its size.
Best targeted using ultra light spin, fly or baitcasting outfits. Will take streamer flies, swimming and surface plugs and small jigs. Baits include live shrimp, pilchard and other baitfish.

Edibility: N/A. Rarely eaten.

Game status: Good. For its size.

STEELHEAD

Scientific name: Ocorhynchus mykiss. Also known as rainbow trout (see separate listing), steelie, chromer, steelhead trout.

Range: Native to the Pacific slopes of Alaska, and south to northern Mexico. Mostly from northern California to Alaska. In the Great Lakes (introduced) where they migrate into the tributary streams to spawn.

Habitat: Steelheads are an anadromous (sea-run) form of rainbow trout. They spend two to three years in the ocean (or Great Lakes) before returning to freshwater streams to spawn.
Tend to hold up in deep pools and behind protective structure when migrating upstream to spawning beds.

Description: In fresh run fish from Great lakes or ocean the coloration is steel blue/green back with bright silver sides and small black spots over the head, upper back, dorsal and tail fin. A feint pink/mauve flash along flank. These colors darken and become duller (closer to non migratory rainbow trout) as fish spend more time in the rivers.

Size: Normally between 10-15 pounds, with some fish doubling these weights.

Tackle and fishing: Fresh run fish are super strong and offer one of the best fights of all the salmonoids. Because of the fish size and strength, top quality tackle is needed when targeting steelies. Fly anglers need to make long casts using big, bright flashy streamer or egg flies. Lure anglers use a variety of flashy spinners and spoons, again with bright colors in their makeup to elicit an aggressive hit.

Salmon egg baits are usually used to entice these spawn run fish.

Edibility: Excellent. With fresh run fish. Dark spawning fish not so much.

Game status: Exceptional. One of the best.

STINGRAY, ATLANTIC

Scientific name: Dasyatis Sabina. Also known as stingaree.

Range: Common North American fish found along the Gulf of Mexico and south-eastern Atlantic coasts as far north as Chesapeake Bay. It roams far upstream in a number of coastal streams during the warmer summer months.

Habitat: Inshore, estuaries and freshwater streams. Freshwater lakes in Florida. Usually over and around sandy shallows and sandbars.

Description: A small stingray with a whip like tail and dangerous barbed spike near the tails base. The body wider than it is long. The snout is relatively long. Coloration is brown or yellow/brown above and fading to lighter towards the outer edges of the disk. Occasionally they have a darker stripe along the centre of the body. White or light gray underneath.

Size: One of the smallest stingrays. Usually a maximum length of around 24 inches and 11 pounds in weight.

Tackle and fishing: Not a spectacular fighter, like al| rays they tend to hold to the bottom and require some effort to lift. Usually taken with light saltwater tackle or heavy freshwater baitcasting or spin gear using cut baits and dead fish. They will eat most bait they come across.

Edibility: Very good.

Game status: Average.

STONECAT

Scientific name: Noturus flavus.

Range: St. Lawrence-Great Lakes, Hudson Bay and Mississippi River basins from Quebec to Alberta in Canada, and south to northern Alabama, northern Mississippi and north eastern Oklahoma. Hudson River drainage New York.

Habitat: Flowing creeks and small to large rivers, throughout rubble and boulder riffles and runs. Gravel areas in lakes.

Description: A flattened head and long, skinny body. Overall yellow/brown/olive with a darker (gray) back and light yellow or white underside.Chin barbels are whitish. Color varies depending on the immediate environment. Can inflict a nasty sting with their dorsal or pectoral spines. The tail is square shaped and the adipose fin merges with the caudal fin and not separated as in the channel catfish or bullhead.

Size: Seldom exceed 8-10 inches in length.

Tackle and fishing: Too small to offer any fight for sport. Usually taken with poles and pieces of natural bait such as grubs and worms, or dough, cheese etc.

Edibility: Fair.

Game status: N/A. Too small

STURGEON, ATLANTIC

Scientific name: Acipenser oxyrhynchus. Also known as common sturgeon.

Range: Labrador, Canada to Florida and west to the Mississippi delta.

Habitat: A long-lived anadromous species that spend most of their life at sea before ascending rivers of their birth to spawn.

Endangered in many locations.

Description: Prehistoric in appearance. Small eyes, mouth on the underside of the head and four barbels on the lower lip. They have an arched back and one row of bony raised plates. Coloring is bluish/black or olive/brown above with paler sides and

STURGEON, ATLANTIC CONTINUED...

a white belly.

Size: Can reach 14 feet and 800 pounds in weight. Males mature at 5 feet and females at 6 feet approximately. They may live up to 100 years.

Tackle and fishing: Strong fighting fish that used to be caught using rigs and baits used for other sturgeon.

Fish numbers are now so depleted that anglers no longer target them.

Edibility: Excellent. No longer killed.

Game status: Excellent. No longer targeted.

STURGEON, GREEN

Scientific name: Acipenser medirostris.

Range: Pacific coast. Coming into rivers to spawn. Not as plentiful as the only other Californian sturgeon, the white sturgeon.

Habitat: In estuaries, bays and lower reaches of rivers.

Description: Amongst the largest and oldest of cartilaginous fishes. They are similar in appearance to white sturgeon except the barbels are closer to the mouth than that of the white sturgeon. Color is green/olive above and lighter below. Highly adapted to feed on the bottom using extremely sensitive barbels on the underside of their snout.

Size: Can grow to 7 feet and 350 pounds. Generally most fish caught are less than 50 pounds.

Tackle and fishing: Not recognised for its fighting ability. What sets it apart is its large size that alone makes it an interesting angling target. Usually caught using heavy baitcasting or lighter saltwater outfits. Takes cut fish bait, clams, shrimp and marine worm baits.

Edibility: Poor.

Game status: Good. Large size makes it a challenge.

STURGEON, LAKE

Scientific name: Acipenser fulvescens. Also known as rock sturgeon.

Range: Great Lakes and the St.Lawrence and Detroit Rivers. Mississippi River drainage system down to Mississippi and Alabama. To the west reaching lake Winnipeg and both the north and south Saskatchewan Rivers. South of Hudson Bay in Canada.

Endangered and extremely rare in many areas. Limited fishing is still available in certain areas with strict size and bag limits.

Habitat: Throughout clear water areas of lakes and rivers. Feeds by sucking up food items found throughout the bottom mud that has been stirred up using its shovel like snout.

Description: An ancient bottom feeding fish. The body is streamlined and covered with rows of bony plates on the back and sides. Coloring is brown overall with a lighter/white belly.

Size: An extremely long living fish that can grow to 7 feet and 240 pounds in weight. Most fish probably average 25 pounds.

IGFA All-Tackle World Record 168 pounds, Georgian Bay, Canada.

Tackle and fishing: A very strong and determined fighter that where legal, is usually caught on heavy baitcast and spin tackle using baits such as worms, crayfish and cut fish baits fished on the bottom.

Edibility: Good.

Game status: Very good.

STURGEON, PALLID

Scientific name: Scaphirhynchus albus.

Range: An endangered fish that is considered imperilled throughout its entire range. Originally found throughout the entire Mississippi and Missouri Rivers. Now found in the lower half of the Mississippi River and the Missouri River.

Habitat: Prefer moderate to swift flowing currents and turbid water between 3-25 feet deep. More common over sandy bottoms in the main channels.

Description: Similar to the shovelnose sturgeon but with a longer pointed snout.

A bottom feeding ancient fish, and one of the largest freshwater fish of North America. Pale in coloring, hence the name, pale gray/white on the back and sides. They become whiter with age.

Size: Can grow to 85 pounds in weight. Length is usually between 30 and 60 inches.

Tackle and fishing: A strong fighter, especially when hooked in strong currents. Usually taken using heavy bottom fishing gear and natural baits such as shellfish, worms, crayfish and mussels.

Edibility: Good. Check regulations before fishing for, or catching/eating.

Game status: Very good. Should be released if caught. Heavy tackle.

STURGEON, SHORTNOSE

Scientific name: Acipenser brevirostrum.

Range: Most major river systems along the eastern seaboard of the United States.

Anadromous fish that spawns in the coastal rivers of the east coast of North America from the St. John River in Canada to the St. Johns River in Florida.

Habitat: Prefer near to shore marine areas, estuaries, and the lower reaches of larger river systems. Habitat destruction has resulted in this fish becoming endangered.

Description: The smallest of the three sturgeons that occur in eastern North America. Coloration is similar to the Atlantic sturgeon with which it shares many waters. Most easily recognised by its short snout.

Size: Grow to 4.7 feet and 50 pounds. Most fish are around 2 feet in length.

Tackle and fishing: A solid fighter that requires strong tackle to subdue. Taken on the bottom using baits such as clams, shrimp, worms and cut fish baits.

Edibility: Good. Should be released.

Game status: Very good. Should be released.

STURGEON, SHOVELNOSE

Scientific name: Scaphirhynchus platorynchus. Also known as river sturgeon, sand sturgeon, switchtail, hackleback.

Range: Much of the Missouri and Mississippi Rivers and larger tributaries. They migrate large distances.

Habitat: Mostly flat, open, swift flowing channels of larger turbid rivers with gravel and sand bottoms. Bottom dwelling fish.

Description: Similar to pallid sturgeon. However the shovelnose has a shorter and less pointed snout that is upturned. Coloring is red/brown or buff. They have scale like plates on the belly and a slender filament (often broken off) running off the tip of the upper tail.

Care should be taking when catching shovelnose to make sure they aren't mistaken for the protected and endangered pallid sturgeon.

Size: Up to 30 inches and 5 pounds. Rarely larger.

Tackle and fishing: Solid little fighters that use the strong currents to their best advantage. Caught on the bottom using worms, crayfish, mussels and other bottom baits.

Edibility: Good.

Game status: Good.

STURGEON, WHITE

Scientific name: Acipenser transmontanus. Also known as Pacific sturgeon, Oregon sturgeon, Californian white sturgeon, Columbia sturgeon, Sacramento sturgeon.

Range: From Alaska along the west coast of North America to central California.

Habitat: Bottom feeding fish that can be found along shorelines, estuaries and bays, and far upstream in suitable rivers. Prefers slow flowing rivers, bays and estuaries including brackish river mouths. Mostly found in marine areas and moving into and up rivers, in faster, clear flowing freshwaters below rapids, gravel and rock structure at spawning time.

Description: Color is gray/brown, pale olive or gray above and clean white below. Fins are dusky gray. It has four barbels near its toothless mouth. Easily identifiable.

Size: The largest freshwater fish of North America. It is known to reach 20 feet in length and weigh 1700 pounds. Generally below 100 pounds.

IGFA All-Tackle World Record 468 pounds, Benicia, CA, USA.

Tackle and fishing: Its sheer size alone makes it a tough adversary. It is a strong fighter that often jumps or rolls on the anglers line to avoid capture. Heavy baitcasting or light saltwater tackle is best used in gentle water, but it may be necessary to go far heavier in fast or deep-water areas. They feed on dead fish, crustaceans, molluscs and baits such as dead shad, smelt anchovies;cut fish, clams, crayfish. Earthworms and shrimp are also effective.

Edibility: Excellent. Anglers should consider releasing all fish even if regulations permit killing. Overfishing and dam construction has reduced the white sturgeon population considerably in many areas.

Game status: Excellent.

SUCKER, BLUE

Scientific name: Cycleptus elongates. Also known as blackhorse, gourdseed sucker, Missouri sucker, bluefish, slenderhead sucker, sweet sucker

Range: Major river systems of the Midwest.

Blue suckers are now rare throughout the Mississippi River basin due to pollution, siltation and the building of dams that has restricted their spring spawning migrations.

Habitat: They prefer deep, swift clear water in pools and channels of large rivers over hard sand, gravel substrate bottoms. Will tolerate turbid water where the current is strong enough to prevent siltation of the pools.

Description: Blue to bluish/gray in color overall and lighter below. They have a small, slender head and a fleshy snout. Thick lips that face downwards. It has a long dorsal fin and forked tail.

Size: Grow to 30 inches and 15 pounds. Most fish caught would be 4-6 pounds or less.

Tackle and fishing: A strong fighting fish that is generally caught with worm baits fished on the bottom.

Edibility: Fair.

Game status: Very good.

SUCKER, FLANNELMOUTH

Scientific name: Catostomus latipinnis

Range: Native to the Colorado River system of the western United States and northern Mexico. The main river of the Colorado River and larger tributaries.

Locally common in areas and under threat in others.

Habitat: A bottom dwelling fish that prefers large rivers where there are slow-flowing deep pools. Found in rocky pools, runs and riffles and margins of rapids. Usually over coarse-gravel bottoms.

Description: Like most suckers, they have fleshy lips located under the snout. Flannelmouth can be identified however by the thickened lower lip that is elongated and divided. Coloration is typically dark green/brown above with orange/yellow flanks and white belly. A long streamlined body.

Size: Most are around 12 inches in length but they can grow to 28 inches.

Tackle and fishing: Not a great fighter. Usually taken when fishing worms or other baits on the bottom.

Edibility: Good

Game status: Fair.

SUCKER, LONGNOSE

Scientific name: Catostomus catostomus. Also known as northern sucker.

Range: Cold waters from Alaska to the Great Lakes and New England. Small populations elsewhere. Widespread throughout northern North America.

Habitat: Mostly deep, cold clear waters of rivers and lakes. Shallower waters during spring spawning.

Description: A long, round body with dark olive/slate gray back and sides and white/yellow belly. They have a long snout and underslung mouth. Breeding males are nearly black on the upper body and head and sometimes have a bright red slash along the flanks. A bottom feeding fish that is often preyed upon by larger predatory fish such as muskellunge, burbot, bass, walleye and northern pike.

Often confused with white suckers. The lower lip of the longnose sucker is larger than that of the white sucker and the scales are smaller.

Size: Typically between 1-2 pounds in weight and 15-25 inches in length.

Tackle and fishing: Not a great fighter. Most are caught using bottom fishing rigs and worms.

Edibility: Good.

Game status: Average.

SUCKER, WHITE

Scientific name: Catostomus commersoni. Also known as common sucker, brook sucker, bay fish, mullet.

Range: The upper Midwest and northeast in North America. As far south as Georgia and New Mexico. Widely distributed.

Habitat: A bottom feeder that is highly adaptable to various habitats. They are relatively tolerant of turbid and polluted waters. Found in small creeks, rivers and lakes, in deep water and shallow shorelines.

Description: A long, round bodied fish that is dark green, dull brown, copper or black on the back and sides with a white belly. During spawning they often show lilac/pink coloration. Fleshy lips under the bottom of the head.

Often confused with the longnose sucker.

They are predated on by walleye, trout, bass, muskellunge etc.

Size: Can reach 12-20 inches and 2-6 pounds. Most are 1 pound or less.

Tackle and fishing: A modest fighter that is usually caught on bottom tackle using worms and other natural insect baits.

Edibility: Poor.

Game status: Poor. Good fish for kids to target.

SUNFISH, GREEN

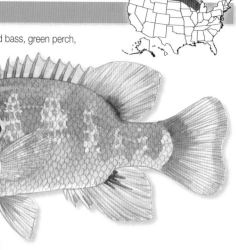

Scientific name: Lepomis cyanellus. Also known as sunny, sand bass, green perch, rubbertail, branch perch.

Range: Native to a wide area of North America east of the Rocky Mountains. Have been introduced to a large number of waters all across the United States.

Habitat: They prefer well-vegetated and snaggy, or rocky areas throughout sluggish backwaters, stream pools, ponds and lakes with sand, gravel or bedrock bottoms. They can live in very turbid and poor quality waters.

Description: Has a larger moth and thicker, longer body than other sunfish. They are more like a warmouth to look at. Body coloration is brown to olive green with bronze/olive green sheen. Lower flanks are yellow/green and belly is pale yellow/white.

Green or blue spots and lines on the gill cover and also a dark spot located near the back end of the dorsal fin, the bases of the anal fins, and on the ear plate.

They are a popular aquarium fish. They can hybridize with other sunfish, which can make identification difficult.

Size: Generally between 4 and 8 ounces. Maximum recorded length is 12 inches.

IGFA All-Tackle World Record 2 pound 2 ounces, Stockton Lake, Missouri, USA.

Tackle and fishing: A very popular sunfish by many anglers because of their co-operative nature. Many are caught by accident when anglers are chasing other species. They can be caught using poles, very light spin or fly tackle and will eat night crawlers, meal worms, waxworms, crickets, horse flies and small minnows, as well as store bought pieces of processed meats etc. They will hit small popping bugs, tiny spinners, marabou jigs, small crankbaits and artificial flies.

Edibility: Very good.

Game status: Poor. Good fish for kids to target.

SUNFISH, LONGEAR

Scientific name: Lepomis megalotis. Also known as redbellied bream, bigear, cherry bream.

Range: Throughout Texas except in the headwaters of the Canadian and Brazos River. As far north and west of Quebec and Minnesota, and down to New Mexico and central Mexico. Not found in most of Florida or along the Atlantic Coast states.

Habitat: Prefers flowing small streams and creeks. Around vegetation, mostly in the pools, backwaters and side channels where it can avoid strong currents. It can be found in some reservoirs.

Description: Similar to the redbreast sunfish. A very pretty fish with an all over brassy coloration, overlaid with patches and streaks of turquoise. Males are frequently scarlet or bright orange in color, also with the blue/turquoise markings on the head. The black, elongated gill cover or opercle flap is what allows quick identification of this fish from other sunfish. This flap is always edged in white in adult fish.

Size: Longears rarely exceed 6 inches in length.

IGFA All-Tackle World Record 1 pound 12 ounces, Elephant Butte Lake, New Mexico, USA.

Tackle and fishing: Another scrappy fighter for its size. They are caught using poles, ultra light spin or fly tackle and are relatively easy to catch with makes them an ideal fish for children to catch. They eat worms and most other small natural baits such as crickets etc. They will aggressively hit small jigs and spinners as well as wet flies and surface poppers. They make good bait for trotliners.

Edibility: Excellent.

Game status: Very good. On ultra light tackle.

SUNFISH, REDBREAST

Scientific name: Lepomis auritus. Also known as redbelly, sun perch, yellowbelly sunfish, red breasted bream, yellowbelly.

Range: Native to the Eastern coast states in streams that drain into the Atlantic Ocean, and introduced into Texas.

Habitat: Flowing streams.

Description: Belly is yellow or orange/ rust color. Similar to other sunfish but with a considerably longer opercle flap than that of even the Longear Sunfish.

Size: One of the larger sunfish. Occasionally reaching one pound or more. Maot average 4- 8 ounces.

Tackle and fishing: They are a very aggressive feeder and give a good fight for their size. They feed on insects, snails, small baitfish and crayfish. They can be caught on worms and crickets also, and will hit plugs meant for bass along with in-line spinners, popping bugs and wet flies.

Edibility: Excellent.

Game status: Excellent for its size.

SUNFISH, REDEAR

Scientific name: Lepomis microlophus. Also known as yellow bream, shellcracker, Georgia bream, sun perch, sunny, cherry gill, rouge ear sunfish.

Range: Originally occurring in south eastern United States from Texas to south Illinois, and east to the Atlantic Ocean. Due to widespread introductions, it is now occurs west into New Mexico and north into Ohio, Michigan and Pennsylvania. Not as widespread as Bluegill however.

Habitat: Usually found near the bottom in deeper water than other sunfish, in warm water and around aquatic vegetation in lakes, reservoirs, ponds, marshy wetlands and streams. They often congregate in groups around vegetation and sunken logs.

Often caught in late spring and early summer when they are concentrated around shallow water areas. The name 'shellcracker' comes about because snails make up a large part of their diet.

Description: Generally resembles a bluegill apart from its larger size and coloring. Dark olive or bluish gray above and on upper sides, and bright yellow/green below on the belly and breast. They often feature feint, dark vertical bars along the flanks. Male fish have a bright, cherry red edge on the operculum, behind the black spot, while female redear have an orange coloration.

Size: Most redear caught are between ½ and 1 pound, and 8 to 10 inches in length. Maximum length is around 17 inches.

IGFA All-Tackle World Record 5 pound 12 ounces, Lake Havasu, Arizona, USA.

Tackle and fishing: Harder to target than other sunfish as they rarely come close to the surface and hit flies or other surface lures. Most are taken on natural baits such as grubs and earthworms fished on the bottom. Anglers do use poles, light spin and fly tackle, but most fish are taken with baits such as worms fished on the bottom. When redears are around spawning beds in shallow waters, both fly and lure anglers do well also.

Edibility: Excellent. Very tasty fillets. White flaky meat.

Game status: Very good.

SUNFISH, SPOTTED

Scientific name: Lepomis punctatus. Also known as stumpknocker, bream.

Range: The Mississippi basin up to central Illinois. Southeast from Florida to Texas and up to North Carolina. More common in the south than the north.

Habitat: Slow (or non) flowing, heavily vegetated ponds, swamps, creeks and streams. Around snags, stumps and ledges over mud, sand and gravel substrates. Breeds in shallow ponds, lakes and creeks.

Description: A thick and ovate body shape. Darker above, olive green to brown with black or reddish spots on the base of each scale which form rows along the flanks. Belly is cream or pale red.

Size: Far less than one pound. Most fish caught are less the ½ pound.

Tackle and fishing: A very aggressive little fish whose fight is limited by its diminutive size. Can be caught in shallow waters throughout most of the year. Poles, ultra light spin and fly tackle are a productive when targeting sunfish. Fishing worms from a pole around stumps and structure rarely fails if these fish are around. Other baits include corn, leeches and grubs; small minnows will work and generally catch the bigger specimens. They are aggressive and will hit most small lures or flies. They are fun and common to catch when ice fishing.

Edibility: Excellent.

Game status: Fun. Too small for serious sport.

TILAPIA, BLACKCHIN

Scientific name: Sarotherodon melanotheron.

Range: A non-native species. Hawaii and both coasts of Florida in the Gulf region.

Habitat: Fresh and brackish habitats in coastal streams, marshes and canals. Prefer backwater habitats with abundant vegetation.

Description: A pale colored fish with variable light blue, orange or golden yellow tonings. Often with irregular bars, spots or blotches around the body and head. A small mouth filled with numerous small teeth.

Size: Most US fish are less than ½ a pound in weight, but they can grow to twice that.

Tackle and fishing: Too small for any real sport. Can be taken with poles or lightweight spin tackle and various baits such as worms, shrimp pieces and cut fish baits.

Edibility: Good.

Game status: Poor. Generally too small.

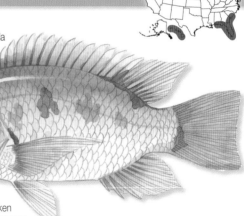

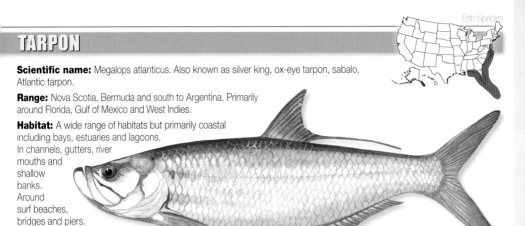

TARPON

Scientific name: Megalops atlanticus. Also known as silver king, ox-eye tarpon, sabalo, Atlantic tarpon.

Range: Nova Scotia, Bermuda and south to Argentina. Primarily around Florida, Gulf of Mexico and West Indies.

Habitat: A wide range of habitats but primarily coastal including bays, estuaries and lagoons. In channels, gutters, river mouths and shallow banks. Around surf beaches, bridges and piers. In brackish and saltwater. Commonly ascend rivers into freshwater habitats.

They prefer water temperatures between 66 F – 86 Fahrenheit.

Description: Upper body greenish blue with bright silver sides. Fish living in brackish water can be more bronze in color. Single dorsal fin with long, rear trailing ray. Dorsal and tail fin often dusky gray color. Lower jaw is protruding, and reaches up and past upper jaw. Fish have extremely bony mouths that resist the penetration of hooks.

Size: Fish are caught from a few pound to 50 plus pound usually with fish around 100 pound not uncommon. Can grow to over 8 feet in length with a maximum weight of 300 pound.

IGFA All-Tackle World Record 283 pound 4 ounces, Sherbro Island, Sierra Leone.

Tackle and fishing: One of the worlds all time greatest sportfish. They perform spectacular leaps interspersed with long, strong runs. In deeper water they will fight very stubbornly and can take hours to subdue. Setting the hook into a tarpons mouth may require numerous strikes and it is also very rough which necessitates the use of heavier shock tippets to avoid cut offs. Selection of tackle is often dependent on size of fish being targeted. When targeting big fish, lines of 30 to 50 pound test may be necessary, while smaller fish can be adequately targeted on 15 pound line.

Trolling with plugs, feather jigs, spoons and natural baits. Spinning with lures and flycasting. Drifting or anchored while fishing live or dead baits such as crabs, shrimp and small fish or dead baits such as full or part mullet and menhaden etc. Prime time to fish baits is often during the night or early morning.

Edibility: Too valuable to eat. Should always be released unharmed if possible.

Game status: Spectacular.

TILAPIA, BLUE

Scientific name: Oreochromis aureas. Also known as Israeli tilapia.

Range: Widespread and abundant throughout Florida and introduced into several other states, including Arizona, Colorado, Texas, Alabama, Nevada and Georgia.

Its introduction to the US has created a number of environmental problems for native fish habitat.

An introduced species native to North and Western Africa and the Middle East.

Habitat: Fertile rivers, ponds, lakes and canals and some inshore marine habitats. A high tolerance to brackish water.

Description: Gray/powder blue shadings on the back and sides with white belly. There are faint vertical bars along flanks and some scattered small spots. The outer borders of the dorsal and caudal fins are red/pink in color.

They are mouthbrooders.

Size: Can reach 10 pounds. Most common between 2-4 pounds in weight.

Tackle and fishing: When hooked on light rod and line (which is rare) it can offer a good fight. It can be caught using worm, pieces of hot dog, bread dough balls and corn kernels. Occasionally taken on artificial lures and flies. Bowhunting for tilapia, where legal, is popular.

Edibility: Excellent. White flaky flesh with a mild flavor.

Game status: N/A. Rarely caught on rod and line.

TILAPIA, MOZAMBIQUE

Scientific name: Tilapia mossambica. Also known as Mozambique mouthbrooder.

Range: Native to tropical and subtropical Africa. Salton Sea in California, Florida, Arizona and Texas in the United States.

Habitat: Occurs in fresh and brackish water where there is plenty of aquatic vegetation. Can survive in water below 50 degrees Fahrenheit and above 100 degrees Fahrenheit.

Description: A deep bodied fish with long dorsal fins. Coloring varies but generally fish are a dull green or yellow with some faint banding.

Size: Adults reach 14 inches and up to 2.5 pounds. Most are less than 1 pound however.

Tackle and fishing: A good little fighter that is taken with poles, light spin and fly tackle. They will eat most natural baits used for panfish plus tiny spinners, jigs, popping bugs and flies.

Edibility: Good.

Game status: Good. On ultra light tackle.

TILAPIA, REDBELLY

Scientific name: Tilapia zillii.

Range: Native to tropical and subtropical Africa. Southern California, southern Arizona and Florida. Cooler water temperatures restrict their range.

Habitat: Salton Sea in California. Invaded ponds, irrigation ditches, drainage canals and streams. They feed on aquatic plants for the most part but will eat crustaceans etc.

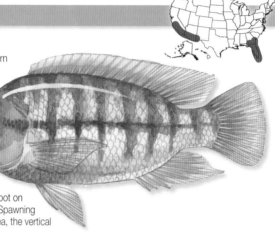

Description: Deep, elongate and laterally compressed body. Coloring is normally dark olive dorsally with lighter olive or brown sides and white or yellow belly. The flanks have an iridescent sheen and 6-7 faint vertical bars. A dark spot on the base of the dorsal fin and at the base of the tail fin. Spawning fish become darker green with a red throat and belly area, the vertical bars become more pronounced.

Size: Most are between 3-5 inches but can grow to 12 inches.

Tackle and fishing: A solid fighter despite its size. Most are caught with poles or light spin tackle. They are sometimes taken with fly tackle. Baits include, dough, worms, insects, and home brews.

Edibility: Very good.

Game status: Good. For its size.

TILAPIA, SPOTTED

Scientific name: Tilapia mariae. Also known as black mangrove cichlid.

Range: A native fish from West Africa. A large non-native population have become established in Florida. It is also found in Nevada and Arizona.

Habitat: A variety of habitats including still and flowing warm water over barren bottoms or rock and debris covered locations in either shallow or deep water. They tend to hang around structure.

Description: Body is dark olive green to palish yellow/gold overall with eight or nine dark vertical bars along the flanks and extending up onto the dorsal fins. There are also a number of spots in between the darker bars running along the lateral line area. Eyes are red in color.

Size: Rarely grow longer than 6 inches in length. Occasionally twice that size.

TILAPIA, SPOTTED CONTINUED....

Tackle and fishing: Not large enough to put up a solid fight but a scrappy fighter none the less. Taken with poles or light spin tackle using dough, worms and other small baits.

Edibility: Good.

Game status: Fair.

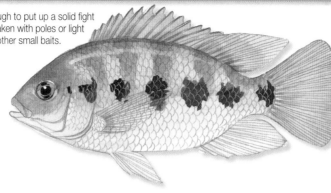

TILAPIA, WAMI

Scientific name: Tilapia urolepis.

Range: A native fish from Africa. Found in California in the United States, but not in the Salton Sea.

Habitat: Brackish and freshwater canals, ponds and ditches. Still and weedy waters.

Description: Silver to steel gray/green with 2-4 lateral blotches.

Size: Rarely larger than 1/2 pound. Can grow to around 3 pound.

Tackle and fishing: A scrappy little fighter that can be caught using poles, light spin or fly tackle. They will hit popping bugs, wet flies, jigs and spinners (small) and the usual baits such as worms and other panfish baits.

Edibility: Good.

Game status: Good.

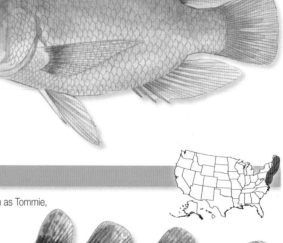

TOMCOD, ATLANTIC

Scientific name: Microgradus tomcod. Also known as Tommie, Tommy cod, winter cod.

Range: Northern Newfoundland to Virginia.

Habitat: Coastal, brackish and freshwater and several landlocked lakes. Around jetties, piers and docks.

Description: Similar in appearance to the Atlantic Cod except the tail and dorsal fins are rounded. Elongated body and small head and pelvic fin has slightly elongated filament. Coloring is olive/brown/yellow dorsally with darker mottling on back and sides. Lower sides and belly pale cream.

Size: Up to 12 inches with a maximum length of around 15 inches.

Tackle and fishing: Not recognised as a fighting fish, it can be caught on all manner of tackle. Ultra-light spin and baitcasting tackle gives anglers the most fun. Will take numerous baits including clams, squid, marine worms, cut fish baits etc.

Edibility: Excellent.

Game status: Poor. Best on ultra light tackle.

TROUT, BROOK

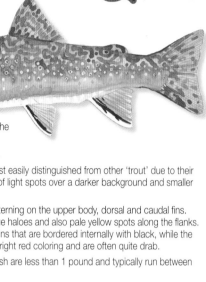

Scientific name: Salvelinus fontinalis. Also known as squaretail, brookie, mountain trout, speckled trout, native trout, brook char.

Range: Native from the Hudson Bay basin, Great Lakes Basin, Atlantic coastal areas from Maine to New Jersey and along the Appalachian chain to northern Georgia. North eastern Canada. Transplanted into other areas and now widely distributed throughout North America and Alaska.

Habitat: Normally associated with rocky, mountain stream habitats with moderate gradients and permanent cold water. Most successful in streams with good overhead forest cover and where the water temperatures are below 68 degrees Fahrenheit.

Sea run brook trout do occur in some Canadian and New England rivers.

Description: A member of the char subgroup of the salmon family. Most easily distinguished from other 'trout' due to their lack of teeth in the roof of their mouth and their coloring, which consists of light spots over a darker background and smaller scales. True trout have lighter background body color with darker spots.

Generally brown/black/olive above with paler yellow/olive 'worm-like' patterning on the upper body, dorsal and caudal fins. Belly and lower jaw is white. There are numerous small red spots with blue haloes and also pale yellow spots along the flanks. On breeding male fish, the pectoral, anal and pelvic fins have white margins that are bordered internally with black, while the remainder of fins are orange/red. Non-breeding fish have less apparent bright red coloring and are often quite drab.

Size: Fish in lakes and big rivers can reach 5-10 pounds. Most stream fish are less than 1 pound and typically run between 6-12 inches.

IGFA All-Tackle World Record 14 pound 8 ounces, Nipigon River, Ontario.

Tackle and fishing: A true sportfish that fights hard but rarely jumps. Can be taken on spin and baitcasting outfits but for the most part targeted by flyfishers using dry, wet and streamer flies. It will hit spoons, spinners and swimming minnows as well as live baits such as worms, crickets, hoppers and live minnows.

Edibility: Excellent.

Game status: Excellent.

TROUT, BROWN

Scientific name: Salmotrutta. Also known as German brown, European brown, brownie, sea trout.

Range: Widely introduced into suitable freshwater environments throughout North America. Also widely in Canada. Sea run forms of brown trout, which are called sea runners, often occur where suitable conditions are found. Brown trout also frequent suitable tidal estuarine systems. All of these fish spawn in freshwater.

Habitat: In coldwater rivers and lakes. They inhabit generally slower, downstream waters than rainbow trout (Oncorhynchusmykiss) but will frequent heavy currents, especially in big rivers. Usually frequenting pools and slower runs in rivers, especially where there is protective overhead, and below water cover, and undercut banks. Lakes and river tailraces below dams. They cannot survive in waters that are highly polluted..

Description: Range in color from silver with few black spots and white bellies (often found in lake fish or sea runners) to golden yellow/brassy or butter brown with pronounced larger black spots and intermittent red spots with lighter or white halos. Coloring can vary greatly between fish even from the same water.

Size: Can grow to 44 pounds or more. Most fish caught in North American streams probably average 1-2 pounds or less, lake fish are generally bigger, perhaps twice that average, while some waters such as the Great Lakesat times produce fish in excess of 20 pounds. Sea run fish are often bigger due to their diet often featuring predominantly small fish.

Tackle and fishing: Often given the title as the best freshwater sportfish in the world. They are strong, dogged fighters, often leaping in an effort to gain their freedom. They are almost the perfect sportfish, they will hit lures, flies and baits. Are renowned for being wary and not easily fooled. Trolling various spoons, plugs, spinners, near the surface and down deep with downriggers

TROUT, BROWN CONTINUED...

is successful on lakes. Fishing dry flies, streamers and wet flies or lures and soft plastics in rivers and lakes are all productive. Light spin cast and fly rods are generally used except when trolling big lures.

Will take natural baits such as live minnows, worms, crickets, grasshoppers and various aquatic food items.

Edibility: Excellent. Particularly good from very clear streams or where fish feed heavily on crustaceans.

Game status: Excellent. One of the best.

TROUT, BULL

Scientific name: Salvelinus confluentus. Also known as western brook trout, rocky Mountain trout, red spotted char.

Range: North western North America, British Columbia, Yukon, Washington, Idaho, northern Nevada and western Montana.

Habitat: Cold coastal and mountain rivers. Deep, cold, high elevation lakes. They require specific habitat demands in waters generally below 55 degrees Fahrenheit. Clean gravel beds, snags and undercut banks and deep pools in large rivers. Can be migratory moving between large rivers and lakes via the ocean, or non-migratory resident fish. Ocean going fish tend to be larger.

Description: A species of char. Similar to Dolly Varden. They have a large head and mouth, hence the name. Coloring is olive green back and sides with pale spots. The ventral fins have white leading edges. The tail isn't deeply forked like the Lake Trout.

Size: Most commonly caught to around 5-8 pound. Can grow to 41 inches and 32 pounds. IGFA All-Tackle World Record 32 pounds, Lake Pend Orielle, ID, USA.

Tackle and fishing: A solid but not overly flashy fighter. Most fish are taken deep in lakes using strong baitcasting or spincasting tackle. Trolling deep with downriggers and lead lines. They will eat live or dead baitfish, cut baits, spoons, diving plugs and streamer flies, all fished very deep for the most part.

Edibility: Very good. Species threatened in many areas.

Game status: Excellent.

TROUT, CUTTHROAT

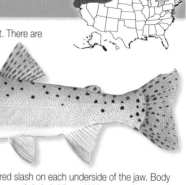

Scientific name: Oncorhynchus clarkii. Also known as red-throated trout, cut. There are several sub species of the cutthroat that have all evolved in different isolated areas.

Range: Native to cold water (freestone) tributaries of the Pacific Ocean, Rocky Mountains and Great Basin in North America. Most mountainous areas south to New Mexico.

Habitat: Usually inhabit and run to spawn in well oxygenated small to large streams with gravel bottoms. Also clear cold lakes and estuaries.Anglers targeting steelhead often catch them.

Description: The common name refers to the very distinctive red/orange colored slash on each underside of the jaw. Body coloration is widely variable. They are similar to stream rainbow trout (that they can and do hybridize with) but are often more ochre in general coloring and have far more black spots over body.

Size: Stream fish are usually less than 1 pound. Anadromous fish from the ocean or lakes can be far bigger.

IGFA All-Tackle World Record 41 pounds, Pyramid Lake, NV, USA.

Tackle and fishing: A solid sportfish with an aggressive nature. They will hit most lures and flies and eat many types of bait. Spin tackle ranges from lightweight for small stream fishing to stouter outfits for big river run fish or when trolling large lakes. Flashy spoons and spinners in sizes to match the water are popular. Fly outfits also vary depending on the water, light lines casting small dry, and wet flies, nymphs and streamers all account for cuts. The bigger sea run and lake fish often hold down at the bottom of large pools and anglers need to get their flies, lures and baits down to them.

Minnows and worms are productive natural baits.

Edibility: Excellent.

Game status: Excellent.

TROUT, GOLDEN

Scientific name: Oncorhynchus (mykiss) aguabonita. A subspecies of rainbow trout that is native to California.

Also known as California golden trout, Kern River trout, volcano creek trout

This species, along with the Little Kern golden trout (O. m. whitei) and the Kern River rainbow trout (O. m. gilberti), all found in the same region, form what is known as the 'golden trout complex".

Range: Native to Golden Trout Creek, which is a tributary of the Kern River, Volcano Creek and the South Fork Kern River.

It has been transplanted to other streams and lakes in the high country areas of California and other western states.

Habitat: High elevations (7-10,000 feet) for the pure strains. Hybrids can be found in rivers and lakes at lower elevations.

Description: An extremely pretty fish. Dorsally olive green fading to golden flanks and pale yellow/orange belly, a red slash along the flanks overlaid with 10 dark vertical oval shaped 'parr' marks. The leading edges of the dorsal, lateral and anal fins are white. Dorsal, adipose and tail fins are spotted. The upper body is lightly spotted.

Size: Generally 6-12 inches in length. Translocated fish have been known to grow to 11 pounds in lakes.

IGFA All-Tackle World Record 11 pounds, Cooks lake, WY, USA.

Tackle and fishing: Typical trout fight. Most fun is had when anglers use ultralight fly and spincasting tackle. Small dry, wet flies and nymphs. Very small spinners.

Edibility: Excellent.

Game status: Excellent.

TROUT, LAKE

Scientific name: Salvelinus namaycush. Also known as mackinaw, laker, gray trout, siscowet, lake char, touladi, togue, paperbelly, lean.

Range: Northern Canada and Alaska, and northern most Lower States. Introduced into some more southern areas.

Habitat: They live in cold, oxygen rich waters. Very deep lakes, often living at depths between 50-200 feet. Sometimes in tributary rivers.

Description: Slate gray to green colored body with paler belly area. The body, head, dorsal and caudal fins are covered in cream colored spots. The tail fin is deeply forked and the lower fins are orange/red in color with white edges.

Size: The largest of the char family. Generally average 24-36 inches in length. Usually between 5-25 pounds. Fish of 15-40 pound aren't uncommon.

IGFA All-Tackle World Record 72 pounds, Great Bear Lake, N.W.T.

Tackle and fishing: A strong if not flashy fighting fish. An important sportfish. Most of the year fish are caught down deep using heavy spin or bait tackle and downriggers or lead lines. At these times the fish will take trolled spoons, diving plugs or live fish baits.

In some areas, particularly in the far northern lakes, but in lower lakes during summer, fish will come in closer to shore and can then be targeted by anglers casting lures as well as flies.

Edibility: Excellent.

Game status: Excellent.

TROUT, RAINBOW

Scientific name: Oncorhynchus mykiss. Also known as steelhead (see separate listing).

Range: Native to coldwater tributaries of the Pacific Slopes of Alaska south to northern Mexico. It has been transplanted across the world. In all US states where trout are found, including Hawaii and Canada.

Habitat: Fastwater streams, rivers and lakes. They can tolerate warmer water than most other trout.

Description: Coloration varies greatly based on habitat and various sub-species. In clear water lakes and large clear rivers the coloration is mostly silvery iridescence with a faint pink stripe along sides. This coloration more closely resembles the 'steelhead'. Rainbows of weedier lakes and smaller streams usually have olive backs down to a bright pink side slash and silver/white lower body/belly area. The upper body, head, dorsal and tail fin is covered in numerous small darker spots.

Colours darken in spawning fish and males develop a kype.

Size: Stream and river fish vary in size depending on the size of the water. Most fish would be around ½ - 1.5 pounds. Lake and big river fish usually grow bigger and can be from 1.5 – 5 pounds. Some lakes (especially those that feature spawning streams) produce fish of double these figures.

IGFA All-Tackle World Record 42 pound 2 ounces, Bell Island, AK.

Tackle and fishing: A true sporting fish that runs hard and performs numerous leaps when hooked. A wide variety of tackle and rigs are suitable for chasing rainbow trout because of their vast range of habitats. Spincasting, baitcasting and flyfishing are used, from ultralight outfits in mountain streams to stouter tackle in big rivers and lakes. Fish feed on the surface and down deep. Flyfishing with dry and wet flies, using floating and sinking lines in rivers and lakes, spincasting or trolling spoons, swimming and diving plugs, spinners.

Baitfishing using a variety natural and artificial baits such as worms, grasshoppers, minnows, corn kernels, marshmallows, artificial baits and salmon eggs.

Edibility: Good to excellent. Depending on water type. Clear mountain stream fish are tops.

Game status: Excellent. A true sportfish.

WARMOUTH

Scientific name: Lepomis gulosus. Also known as goggle-eye, warmouth perch, stump knocker, mud bass, redeye, molly, rock bass, open-mouth, red-eyed bream.

Range: Great Lakes and Mississippi River basins, from western Pennsylvania to Minnesota, and south to the Gulf of Mexico.

Habitat: Can tolerate murkier waters than most other sunfish. Inhabit lakes, marshes, ponds and swamps; slow flowing sloughs and backwaters with muddy bottoms, stumps, brush and other vegetation.

Description: A thick bodied, large mouthed fish that is similar in appearance to (and often confused with) rock bass and green sunfish. The coloration of adult fish is all over dark mottled brown (even black) with a gold colored belly. Male fish have a bright orange/red spot at the base of the dorsal fin, and often a similar color on the gill flaps. They have three to five prominent red/brown (dark) streaks radiating out from the eyes.

Size: Usually between 6-10 inches, rarely reaches 1 pound in weight, but can grow bigger than 12 inches and weigh up to 2 pound.

IGFA All-Tackle World Record 2 pound 7 ounces, Guess Lake, Holt, FL, USA.

Tackle and fishing: A popular angling species, they hit hard, are very aggressive, and are easily caught using poles, light spin of fly tackle. Natural baits include worms, insects and particularly small minnows. Small jigs and minnow lures are favorites, as are popping bugs with fly anglers.

Edibility: Very good. If caught in clear water. Flesh can have a strong flavor because they are bottom feeders.

Game status: Very good. Too small for any real fight.

WHITEFISH, LAKE

Scientific name: Coregonus clupeaformis. Also known as gizzard fish, eastern whitefish, common whitefish, high back.

Range: Throughout much of Canada, parts of the northern United States, including the Great Lakes.

Habitat: A cool water fish found mostly in deep water in lakes across its southern range. Northern region fish come closer in around the shallows and into streams. Known to also enter brackish water.

Description: Similar to other whitefishes in general appearance. They have an adipose fin similar to other salmonoids. A deep, long bodied fish with a small blunt head and overhanging snout to allow for feeding along the bottom. They have two small flaps on each nostril.

Overall color is typically silver with olive, pale green or brown dorsally. The belly is white and the tails has a dark posterior edge.

Size: Most are around 1 pound but fish can commonly reach 4 pounds.

IGFA All-Tackle World Record 14 pound 6 ounces, Meaford, Ontario.

Tackle and fishing: A game little fighter, especially on light spin, fly or crappie tackle. A simple line and small jig is enough to catch these fish. Ice fishing is popular during the winter months. They will take spinners and spoons, small live fish and cut fish pieces, fly anglers can catch them using dry and wet flies.

Edibility: Excellent. Delicate and delicious flesh and the roe are valued as caviar.

Game status: Good. Often hard to target because of water depth. Becoming more popular with recreational anglers.

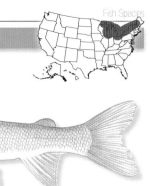

WHITEFISH, MOUNTAIN

Scientific name: Prosopium williamsoni. Also known as Rocky Mountain whitefish.

Range: One of the most widely distributed salmonoids of western North America. From Ontario and Lake Superior to the Border States and New England. Northern Canada and Alaska.

Habitat: Clear cold water mountain streams and lakes. Deep river pools and deepwater lakes. They are bottom feeders and eat snails, amphipods, crayfish and insect larvae.

Description: A slender body, cylindrical in cross section. The head is short with a small underslung mouth. A short dorsal fin and forked tail. All over silver with a dusky green/olive/brown back.

Size: Can grow to 28 inches. Most fish are between 10-16 inches and are 1 pound or less.

IGFA All-Tackle World Record 5 pound 8 ounces, Elbow River, Manitoba.

Tackle and fishing: A good fighter despite many trout anglers looking down on them as non-sportfish. Usually taken on light spin tackle by anglers using salmon eggs and worms for bait, but they will hit tiny spinners as well. Fly anglers usually take them on small nymphs, streamers and occasionally dry flies when targeting trout.

Edibility: Very good.

Game status: Very good. Underrated.

WHITEFISH, ROUND

Scientific name: Prospium cylindraceum. Also known as round fish, pilot fish, frost fish, menominee, menominee whitefish.

Range: From Alaska in the north west to Labrador and New England in the east. Other than Lake Erie, in the Great Lakes.

Now protected in some states.

Habitat: Mostly in cold deep lakes, but throughout many streams and lakes in northern Canada.

Description: Very similar to the mountain whitefish in appearance, but with a more rounded body and pointier head. The head is small in comparison to the length of the body. Coloration is olive/brown dorsally with light silver sides and belly.

Size: Generally between 9-12 inches in length and 1 pound or less in weight. Can grow to around 5 pounds.

IGFA All-Tackle World Record 6 pounds, Putahow River, Manitoba.

Tackle and fishing: Another bottom feeder that mostly eats crustaceans, fish eggs and insect larvae. They are a good little fighter on ultralight/light spin or fly tackle. Lake fish are susceptible to small spinners tipped with natural baits, salmon eggs or maggots. Fly anglers catch them with small nymphs or wet flies in streams.

Edibility: Very good.

Game status: Very good. On very light tackle.

RIGS Bass

CAROLINA WORM RIGS

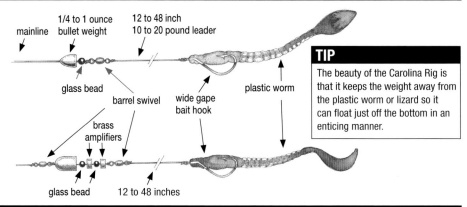

1/4 to 1 ounce
bullet weight

12 to 48 inch
10 to 20 pound leader

mainline

glass bead

barrel swivel

wide gape
bait hook

plastic worm

brass
amplifiers

glass bead

12 to 48 inches

TIP

The beauty of the Carolina Rig is that it keeps the weight away from the plastic worm or lizard so it can float just off the bottom in an enticing manner.

VERTICAL CAROLINA RIG

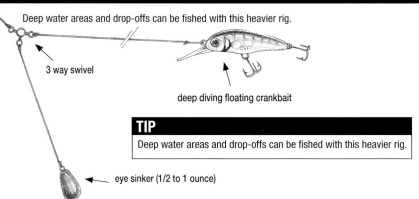

Deep water areas and drop-offs can be fished with this heavier rig.

3 way swivel

deep diving floating crankbait

eye sinker (1/2 to 1 ounce)

TIP

Deep water areas and drop-offs can be fished with this heavier rig.

TEXAS RIGS

free sliding bullet weight

TOPWATER BAITS

CRANKBAIT

SPLIT SHOT RIG

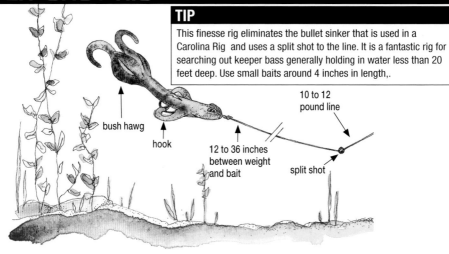

TIP

This finesse rig eliminates the bullet sinker that is used in a Carolina Rig and uses a split shot to the line. It is a fantastic rig for searching out keeper bass generally holding in water less than 20 feet deep. Use small baits around 4 inches in length,.

bush hawg

hook

10 to 12 pound line

12 to 36 inches between weight and bait

split shot

DROP SHOT RIGS

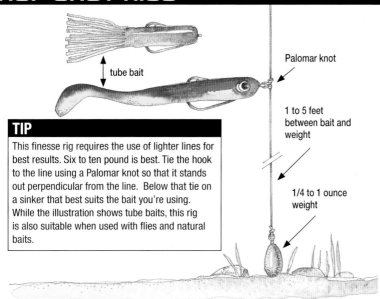

tube bait

Palomar knot

1 to 5 feet between bait and weight

1/4 to 1 ounce weight

TIP

This finesse rig requires the use of lighter lines for best results. Six to ten pound is best. Tie the hook to the line using a Palomar knot so that it stands out perpendicular from the line. Below that tie on a sinker that best suits the bait you're using. While the illustration shows tube baits, this rig is also suitable when used with flies and natural baits.

SPINNER BAITS

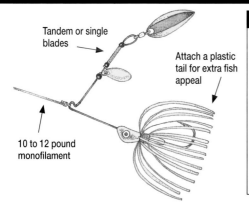

Tandem or single blades

Attach a plastic tail for extra fish appeal

10 to 12 pound monofilament

TIP

Spinnerbaits are very versatile and very productive when it comes to catching bass. Directly attach the line to the spinnerbait being used and when fishing for bass try and always keep in visual contact with the lure and don't strike immediately when a bass hits.
Tandem blades can be fished slower and hold higher in the water and gives off more flash than a single blade which does produce more vibration when it's working.
Consider using a 3 inch plastic trailer to the hook to give extra fish appeal!

RIGS Walleye

LEECH RIG

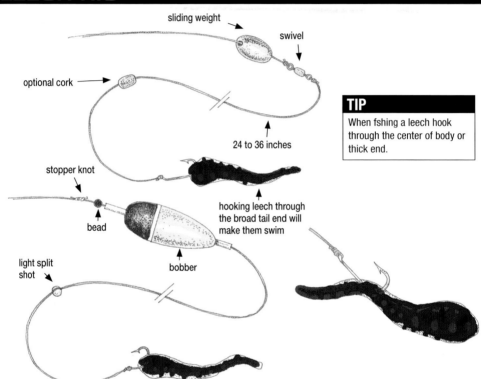

sliding weight

swivel

optional cork

TIP

When fshing a leech hook through the center of body or thick end.

24 to 36 inches

stopper knot

bead

hooking leech through the broad tail end will make them swim

light split shot

bobber

BOTTOM WALKING RIG

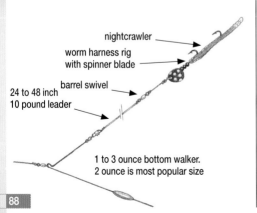

nightcrawler

worm harness rig with spinner blade

barrel swivel

24 to 48 inch 10 pound leader

1 to 3 ounce bottom walker. 2 ounce is most popular size

STAND UP JIG AND NIGHTCRAWLER

TIP

Stand-up Jigs are ideal for both largemouth and smallmouth bass, and when fished with a tube bait (or other soft plastics) they offer a fantastic representation of a defensive crawfish. Add a nightcrawler onto a trailing hook and fish it on a hard rocky bottom or next to a well defined weedbed and get ready for some serious action!

8 to 12 pound line

3/8 to 1 ounce jig head

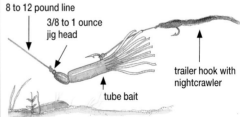

trailer hook with nightcrawler

tube bait

RIGS Crappie & other Panfish

DOUBLE SPREADER RIG

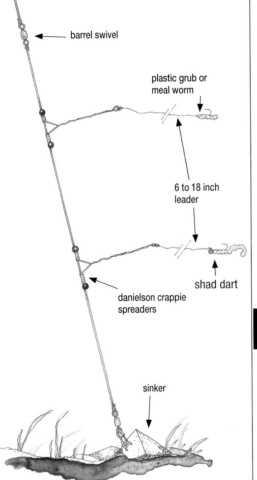

barrel swivel

plastic grub or meal worm

6 to 18 inch leader

shad dart

danielson crappie spreaders

sinker

TIP

Any number of artificial and natural baits work for catching crappie. Small jigs in the ¼ ounce range are very effective as are small minnow baits (live bait or artificial) and small plastic grubs. Keeping a tight line is important to avoid the fish getting off when hooked. Always concentrate on fishing the lure or live bait at the best depth for the time of year and time of day.

JIG AND FLOAT RIG BOBBER AND MEAL WORM RIG

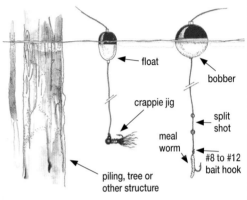

float

bobber

crappie jig

split shot

meal worm

#8 to #12 bait hook

piling, tree or other structure

TIP

Adjust the depth of the hook or jig to match the depth of water and where the fish are holding. Use a few split shots on the line below the float to get light baits into the strike zone or where there might be some current.

DOUBLE BEAR PAW RIG

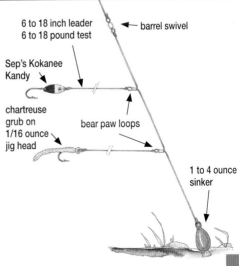

6 to 18 inch leader
6 to 18 pound test

barrel swivel

Sep's Kokanee Kandy

chartreuse grub on 1/16 ounce jig head

bear paw loops

1 to 4 ounce sinker

RIGS Pike-Pickerel & other large gamefish

WEEDLESS SPOON RIGS

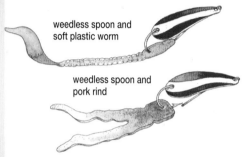

weedless spoon and soft plastic worm

weedless spoon and pork rind

WEEDLESS LIVE BAIT RIG

cigar float

weedless hook

hook live minnow through lips

split shot

TIP

Using a cigar float and weedless hook allows you to fish through surface weed vegetation with less chance of getting snagged.

BOTTOM BUMPING RIG

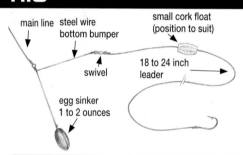

main line steel wire bottom bumper

small cork float (position to suit)

swivel

18 to 24 inch leader

egg sinker 1 to 2 ounces

TIP

This rig with the addition of the cork can be used to keep the bait off the bottom when targeting smallmouth bass and catfish.

QUICK SET RIG

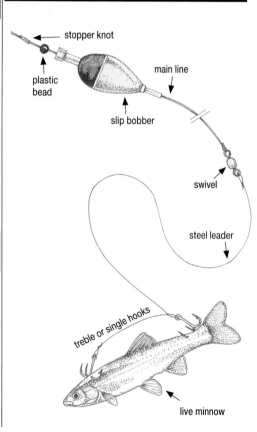

stopper knot

plastic bead

main line

slip bobber

swivel

steel leader

treble or single hooks

live minnow

CONTROLLED-DEPTH LIVE BAIT RIG

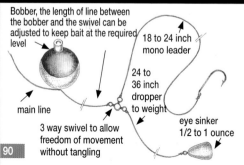

Bobber, the length of line between the bobber and the swivel can be adjusted to keep bait at the required level

18 to 24 inch mono leader

24 to 36 inch dropper to weight

main line

eye sinker 1/2 to 1 ounce

3 way swivel to allow freedom of movement without tangling

RIGS Sturgeon

SLIDER WITH SHRIMP RIG

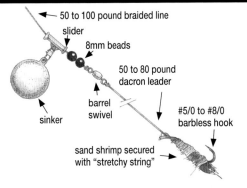

- 50 to 100 pound braided line
- slider
- 8mm beads
- 50 to 80 pound dacron leader
- barrel swivel
- sinker
- #5/0 to #8/0 barbless hook
- sand shrimp secured with "stretchy string"

SLIDER RIG WITH HALF HITCHED SMELT

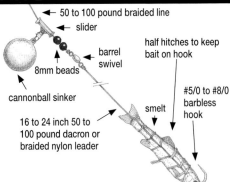

- 50 to 100 pound braided line
- slider
- barrel swivel
- half hitches to keep bait on hook
- 8mm beads
- cannonball sinker
- 16 to 24 inch 50 to 100 pound dacron or braided nylon leader
- smelt
- #5/0 to #8/0 barbless hook

SEWN SHAD STURGEON RIG

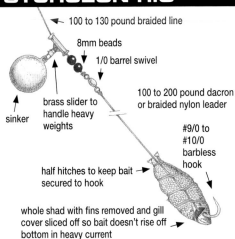

- 100 to 130 pound braided line
- 8mm beads
- 1/0 barrel swivel
- 100 to 200 pound dacron or braided nylon leader
- brass slider to handle heavy weights
- sinker
- #9/0 to #10/0 barbless hook
- half hitches to keep bait secured to hook
- whole shad with fins removed and gill cover sliced off so bait doesn't rise off bottom in heavy current

BANK BREAKAWAY RIG

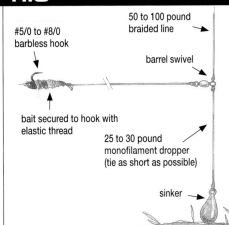

- 50 to 100 pound braided line
- #5/0 to #8/0 barbless hook
- barrel swivel
- bait secured to hook with elastic thread
- 25 to 30 pound monofilament dropper (tie as short as possible)
- sinker

SOFT BOTTOM ESTUARY RIG

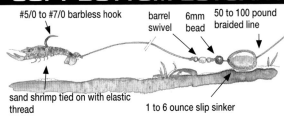

- #5/0 to #7/0 barbless hook
- barrel swivel
- 6mm bead
- 50 to 100 pound braided line
- sand shrimp tied on with elastic thread
- 1 to 6 ounce slip sinker

TIP

Where the bottom is mostly mud and sand, a basic running sinker rig is all that is required, and it's a simple rig to tie. The weight of the sinker you use should be determined by the strength of the tidal current.

RIGS Salmon

Ocean, Estuary and Bay Trolling Rigs

DELTA DIVER & SALMON BUNGEE

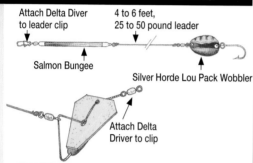

Attach Delta Diver to leader clip

4 to 6 feet, 25 to 50 pound leader

Salmon Bungee

Silver Horde Lou Pack Wobbler

Attach Delta Driver to clip

TIP

Delta Divers are a great way of keeping lures in the strike zone and are a must- have in any salmon anglers trolling arsenal, while a Salmon Bungee between the diver and lure allows fish to take the lure and effectively hook themselves without snapping the rig. There are a wide variety of wobblers, spoons and spinners available for use on this rig setup.

DELTA DIVER & SPINNER RIG

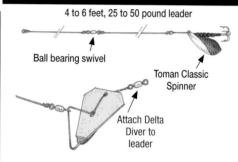

4 to 6 feet, 25 to 50 pound leader

Ball bearing swivel

Toman Classic Spinner

Attach Delta Diver to leader

TIP

Delta Divers are a great way of keeping baits in the strike zone and are a must-have in any salmon anglers trolling arsenal. The addition of a ball-bearing swivel helps eliminate line twists when using spinners.

SPIN-N-GLO RIG

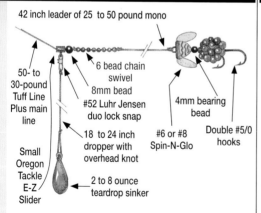

42 inch leader of 25 to 50 pound mono

50- to 30-pound Tuff Line Plus main line

6 bead chain swivel

8mm bead

#52 Luhr Jensen duo lock snap

4mm bearing bead

Small Oregon Tackle E-Z Slider

18 to 24 inch dropper with overhead knot

#6 or #8 Spin-N-Glo

Double #5/0 hooks

2 to 8 ounce teardrop sinker

TIP

One of the most effective rigs for Back Bouncing is using a Spin-N-Glo rig as shown here.

BASIC PLUNKING RIG

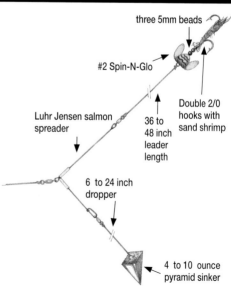

three 5mm beads

#2 Spin-N-Glo

Luhr Jensen salmon spreader

Double 2/0 hooks with sand shrimp

36 to 48 inch leader length

6 to 24 inch dropper

4 to 10 ounce pyramid sinker

DEEPWATER BOBBER FLOAT RIG

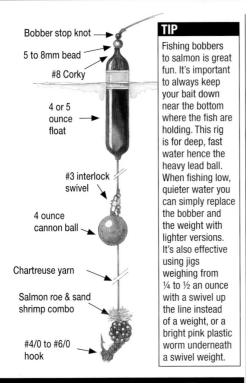

Bobber stop knot

5 to 8mm bead

#8 Corky

4 or 5 ounce float

#3 interlock swivel

4 ounce cannon ball

Chartreuse yarn

Salmon roe & sand shrimp combo

#4/0 to #6/0 hook

TIP

Fishing bobbers to salmon is great fun. It's important to always keep your bait down near the bottom where the fish are holding. This rig is for deep, fast water hence the heavy lead ball. When fishing low, quieter water you can simply replace the bobber and the weight with lighter versions. It's also effective using jigs weighing from ¼ to ½ an ounce with a swivel up the line instead of a weight, or a bright pink plastic worm underneath a swivel weight.

ANCHORED BOAT RIG

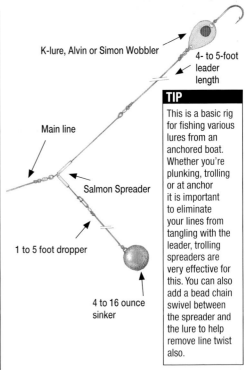

K-lure, Alvin or Simon Wobbler

4- to 5-foot leader length

Main line

Salmon Spreader

1 to 5 foot dropper

4 to 16 ounce sinker

TIP

This is a basic rig for fishing various lures from an anchored boat. Whether you're plunking, trolling or at anchor it is important to eliminate your lines from tangling with the leader, trolling spreaders are very effective for this. You can also add a bead chain swivel between the spreader and the lure to help remove line twist also.

BACK BOUNCING PLUGS

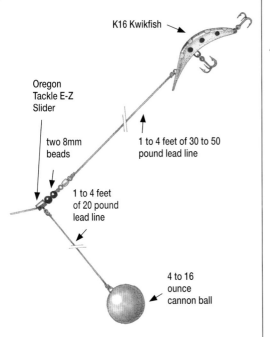

K16 Kwikfish

Oregon Tackle E-Z Slider

two 8mm beads

1 to 4 feet of 30 to 50 pound lead line

1 to 4 feet of 20 pound lead line

4 to 16 ounce cannon ball

BASIC PRAWN TROLLING RIG

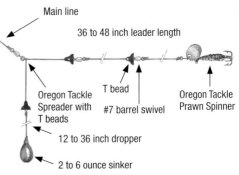

Main line

36 to 48 inch leader length

Oregon Tackle Spreader with T beads

T bead

#7 barrel swivel

Oregon Tackle Prawn Spinner

12 to 36 inch dropper

2 to 6 ounce sinker

TIP

There are many ways of rigging Prawn Troll Rigs, this setup is very easy and productive.

RIGS *Steelhead*

PENCIL LEAD CINCH

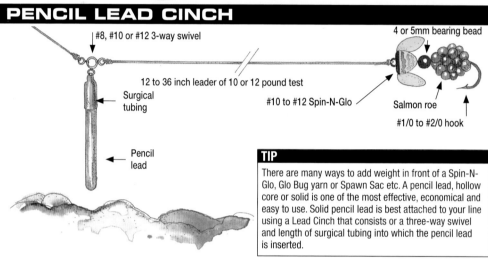

#8, #10 or #12 3-way swivel

4 or 5mm bearing bead

12 to 36 inch leader of 10 or 12 pound test

Surgical tubing

#10 to #12 Spin-N-Glo

Salmon roe

#1/0 to #2/0 hook

Pencil lead

TIP

There are many ways to add weight in front of a Spin-N-Glo, Glo Bug yarn or Spawn Sac etc. A pencil lead, hollow core or solid is one of the most effective, economical and easy to use. Solid pencil lead is best attached to your line using a Lead Cinch that consists or a three-way swivel and length of surgical tubing into which the pencil lead is inserted.

DOUBLE HOOK SIDE-DRIFTING RIG AND SLINKY

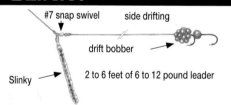

#7 snap swivel   side drifting

drift bobber

Slinky   2 to 6 feet of 6 to 12 pound leader

TIP

Side Drifting baits down to steelhead in a natural manner is often the key to getting a bite. It is a relatively easy method to master and there are a number of side drifting rigs in use. The one shown using a drift bobber and double hooks is very popular.

FLOAT FISHING RIGS

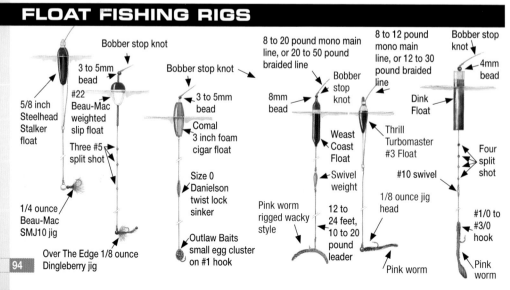

Bobber stop knot

3 to 5mm bead

5/8 inch Steelhead Stalker float

#22 Beau-Mac weighted slip float

Three #5 split shot

1/4 ounce Beau-Mac SMJ10 jig

Over The Edge 1/8 ounce Dingleberry jig

Bobber stop knot

3 to 5mm bead

Comal 3 inch foam cigar float

Size 0 Danielson twist lock sinker

Outlaw Baits small egg cluster on #1 hook

8 to 20 pound mono main line, or 20 to 50 pound braided line

8mm bead

Weast Coast Float

Swivel weight

Pink worm rigged wacky style

12 to 24 feet, 10 to 20 pound leader

8 to 12 pound mono main line, or 12 to 30 pound braided line

Bobber stop knot

Dink Float

Thrill Turbomaster #3 Float

#10 swivel

1/8 ounce jig head

Pink worm

Bobber stop knot

4mm bead

Four split shot

#1/0 to #3/0 hook

Pink worm

DIVER AND BAIT RIGS

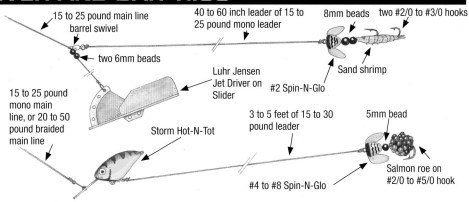

15 to 25 pound main line
barrel swivel

40 to 60 inch leader of 15 to 25 pound mono leader

8mm beads   two #2/0 to #3/0 hooks

two 6mm beads

Sand shrimp

15 to 25 pound mono main line, or 20 to 50 pound braided main line

Luhr Jensen Jet Driver on Slider   #2 Spin-N-Glo

Storm Hot-N-Tot

3 to 5 feet of 15 to 30 pound leader   5mm bead

Salmon roe on #2/0 to #5/0 hook

#4 to #8 Spin-N-Glo

SIDE-PLANER RIGS

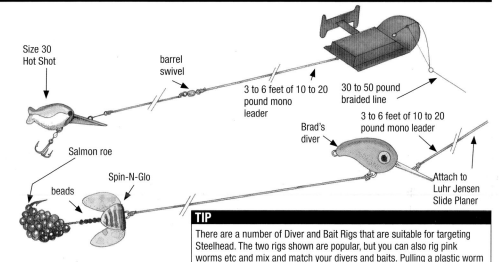

Size 30 Hot Shot

barrel swivel

3 to 6 feet of 10 to 20 pound mono leader

30 to 50 pound braided line

Salmon roe

Brad's diver

3 to 6 feet of 10 to 20 pound mono leader

Spin-N-Glo

beads

Attach to Luhr Jensen Slide Planer

TIP

There are a number of Diver and Bait Rigs that are suitable for targeting Steelhead. The two rigs shown are popular, but you can also rig pink worms etc and mix and match your divers and baits. Pulling a plastic worm behind a diver is a great way to catch steelhead.

SPAWN SAC RIG

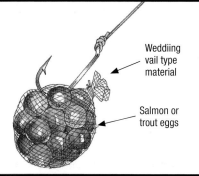

Weddiing vail type material

Salmon or trout eggs

TIP

You can make a Spawn Sac Rig by taking 10 or so salmon or trout eggs and creating a 'parcel' of eggs using any 'wedding vail' type material and then fishing it under a float or bottom drift rig.

PINK PLASTIC WORM RIG

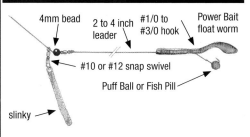

4mm bead   2 to 4 inch leader   #1/0 to #3/0 hook   Power Bait float worm

#10 or #12 snap swivel

Puff Ball or Fish Pill

slinky

TIP

Steelhead love plastic worms, and one of the best snag resistant rigs is a slinky sinker setup with a 4-6 inch worm. You can also run the worm upside down or 'half wacky' style to give the rig more action and fish pulling power.

RIGS Trout and Kokanee Rigs

TROLLING RIG

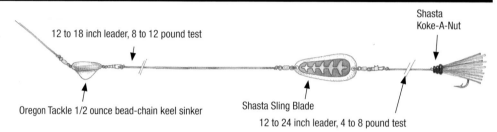

Shasta Koke-A-Nut

12 to 18 inch leader, 8 to 12 pound test

Oregon Tackle 1/2 ounce bead-chain keel sinker

Shasta Sling Blade

12 to 24 inch leader, 4 to 8 pound test

TIP

While flyfishing for Kokanee cruising shorelines can be successful in spring. By far the most productive method is by trolling the open water. Trolling very slowly while using your boats electronics to locate schools of fish is generally successful. Using dodgers and flashers to attract both Kokanee and trout is successful.

BOTTOM RIG

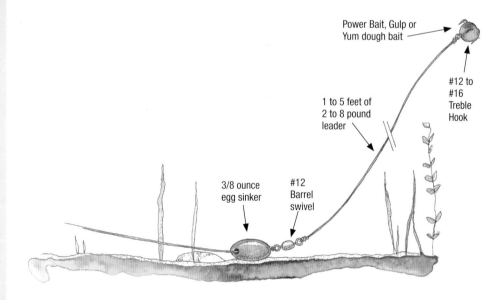

Power Bait, Gulp or Yum dough bait

#12 to #16 Treble Hook

1 to 5 feet of 2 to 8 pound leader

3/8 ounce egg sinker

#12 Barrel swivel

TIP

Power baits are fantastic for fishing up off the bottom and above the weed. Any cruising trout, especially rainbows find it hard to resist a brightly colored artificial bait. These baits can also be used on dropper rigs when fishing a tight line back to the rod.

FLOAT RIGS

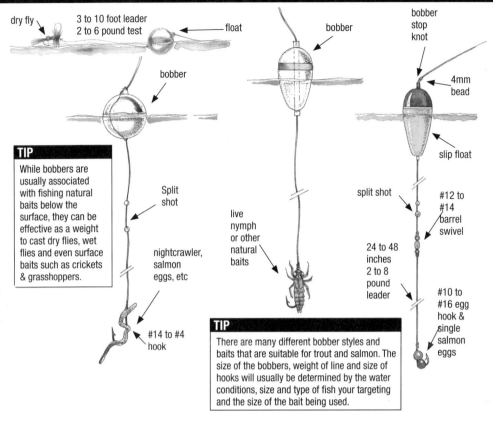

dry fly

3 to 10 foot leader
2 to 6 pound test

float

bobber

bobber
stop
knot

bobber

bobber

4mm
bead

slip float

TIP

While bobbers are usually associated with fishing natural baits below the surface, they can be effective as a weight to cast dry flies, wet flies and even surface baits such as crickets & grasshoppers.

Split shot

nightcrawler, salmon eggs, etc

#14 to #4 hook

live nymph or other natural baits

split shot

24 to 48 inches 2 to 8 pound leader

#12 to #14 barrel swivel

#10 to #16 egg hook & single salmon eggs

TIP

There are many different bobber styles and baits that are suitable for trout and salmon. The size of the bobbers, weight of line and size of hooks will usually be determined by the water conditions, size and type of fish your targeting and the size of the bait being used.

DOWN RIGGER SETUPS

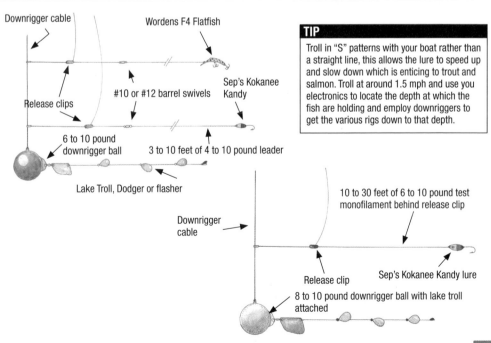

Downrigger cable

Wordens F4 Flatfish

Sep's Kokanee Kandy

#10 or #12 barrel swivels

Release clips

6 to 10 pound downrigger ball

3 to 10 feet of 4 to 10 pound leader

Lake Troll, Dodger or flasher

TIP

Troll in "S" patterns with your boat rather than a straight line, this allows the lure to speed up and slow down which is enticing to trout and salmon. Troll at around 1.5 mph and use you electronics to locate the depth at which the fish are holding and employ downriggers to get the various rigs down to that depth.

10 to 30 feet of 6 to 10 pound test monofilament behind release clip

Downrigger cable

Release clip

Sep's Kokanee Kandy lure

8 to 10 pound downrigger ball with lake troll attached